All My Children Wear Fur Coats
How to Leave a Legacy for Your Pet

Peggy R. Hoyt, J.D., M.B.A.

*For all
your children
who wear
fur coats!*
PRHoyt

Foreword by John A. Hoyt, former President and CEO,
The Humane Society of the United States, 1970-1997

ii

Dedication

This book is dedicated to all of my fur-faced children—

past, present and future

A portion of the proceeds of this book will be

donated to The Humane Society of the United States,

as well as other animal-centered charities.

For more information or to order a copy of this book,
visit www.legacyforyourpet.com or contact
The Law Offices of Hoyt & Bryan, LLC
251 Plaza Drive, Suite B, Oviedo, Florida 32765
Phone (407) 977-8080 ▪ Facsimile (407) 977-8078 ▪ www.hoytbryan.com.

Cover Design by Kimberly D'Angelo, Archer-Ellison/bookcovers.com
Interior Design by Julie Hoyt Dorman

Contents

v

5/03

6

Animal Care Organizations

page 89

7

Choosing an Estate Planning Attorney

page 103

8

Ways to Memorialize Your Pet

page 123

9

Pet Loss and Grief Therapy

page 131

10

Pet Memories

page 153

Acknowledgements

I would like to express my gratitude and appreciation to my pets for allowing me the privilege of sharing in their lives and for providing the inspiration for this book. I want to thank both my fiance, Joe Allen, and my partner, Randy Bryan, for persevering with me through this project and not giving up on my "crazy" ideas. I am grateful to all of my friends and colleagues who assisted me, participated in the project, and provided me with reference material, sample language, editorial advice and encouragement. I want to specifically acknowledge my dear friends Lisa Senecal and Marguerite Longoria, my veterinarian Dr. Edward Griffith and everyone who works with me at The Law Offices of Hoyt & Bryan, LLC. I am thankful for the guidance of the National Network of Estate Planning Attorneys, Lifespan™ Legal Services, LLC and their collective leaders and members. Many of the ideas, philosophies and education were obtained through these people and organizations. I am appreciative of Paul Irwin and The Humane Society of the United States for their willingness to believe in this project as an extension of the excellent work they are already doing in the field of animal welfare. And last, but certainly not least, I could not have done any of this without my sister, Julie Hoyt Dorman, and my father, John A. Hoyt. Both of them were instrumental in providing insight, creativity and support for the layout, design and content of this book.

NOTES

Foreword

Most people love and care for their pets—most of the time. Those who don't are quite often those who acquire or breed animals for commercial or recreational purposes. In such cases, the word "pet" is probably inappropriate and even more so the term "companion animal." Animals regarded as pets or companions are animals that are acquired to be loved rather than possessed as a means for commercial gain or self-gratifying utility.

All My Children Wear Fur Coats is a book for those persons who regard animals as companions—members of the family. Whether a cat or dog, a horse or bird, most companion animals are regarded as an integral and intimate part of a larger family of human beings or an individual human with whom they share relationships. It is these animals especially who are at the center of *All My Children Wear Fur Coats*, animals for whom care and companionship are paramount.

Peggy Hoyt has combined her intense love for animals and her nationally recognized skills as an attorney concentrating in trusts and estates to help individuals plan for the continuing care and welfare of their pet or pets, especially persons who are elderly or facing long-term illness or disablement. *All My Children Wear Fur Coats* addresses with sensitivity and insight the importance of pets in the lives of their human companions, and ways in which such persons can honor and remember their pets both during their respective lifetimes and beyond.

As the father of the author of this book, I take great pride in the legacy my daughter Peggy demonstrates in this book and the ways in which her skill and insight can assist each of us in honoring and providing for those non-human members of our families, creatures whose need for love and care may well extend beyond our ability to provide it personally.

Most people love and care for their pets most of the time. But most of us have given little thought to their care beyond our ability to provide such care personally. After reading this book, you will have a blueprint for ensuring that the love and care you now provide your pet will be continued for as long as your pet lives.

All My Children Wear Fur Coats is a book of celebration and remembrance!

—*John A. Hoyt,*
former President and Chief Executive Officer,
The Humane Society of the United States

Preface

This book is written for people who love pets and for people who consider their pets to be members of their family, even their "children." It is an effort to share some thoughts and ideas with people who are concerned about the day when they may lose their pet or their pet may lose them—either to disability or to death.

September 11, 2001, means different things to different people. For me, as an estate planning attorney, it focused some of my concern not just on the planning (or lack thereof) that we leave for our human families but also on the plans that we have considered or implemented for our "children who wear fur coats." I am convinced we are all woefully unprepared.

All of my children do wear fur coats. I have no human children, only pets. I am like thousands of other people in America whose world revolves around the day-to-day concerns of neighs, barks, chirps and meows. The concerns and ideas depicted in this book are concerns that I share. They are also concerns that I am dedicated to sharing with others and toward which I am working to improve in my professional career. My dream is to serve animals through the creation, administration and operation of the All Horses Go To Heaven Ranch, a not-for-profit organization dedicated to the perpetual care of all horses, but specifically wild Mustangs. Hopefully, my law practice and this book will someday make this dream possible.

I invite you to read this book with an open mind. It is not designed as an exhaustive treatise or the last word on the subject of estate planning or charitable giving. It is intended for people who have an interest in the subject and would like to either learn more or continue to make a difference in the lives of pets—not just their pets, but all the pets of the world. If you know someone who would benefit from the information, please help spread the word.

I welcome your comments, your questions and your concerns regarding the subject matter. If I cannot help you, I will do my best to find someone who can.

Pet Ownership in America Today

A mericans love pets! The American Pet Products Man-ufacturers Association (APPMA) 2001-2002 National Pet Owner's Survey reports that people in the United States own a total of 141 million dogs and cats. There are approximately 68 million dogs and 73 million cats living in our homes and in our hearts. Many of these pet households have multiple pets: 24 percent of dog owners have two or more dogs and 51 percent of cat owners have two or more cats. About 20 percent of the reported pets were adopted from an animal shelter.

In my home there are three horses (Reno, Tahoe and Sierra), three cats (Beijing, Cuddles and Bangle) and three dogs (Buddy, Kira and Corkie). All of my horses are adopted through various rescue programs, including the Bureau of Land Management's Wild Horse and Burro Program and an adoption program which rescues foals from slaughterhouse auctions after they have been discarded by Premarin farms in Canada. Two of my three cats were shelter orphans, and my dog Kira is from an Orlando, Florida, rescue organization. My remaining "kids" were family hand-me-downs, gifts or charity cases.

However, dogs and cats are not our only choice for animal companionship. Just as Americans have diverse tastes in television programs, cars and music, we also have wide variations in our choices for pets we call "children." Outside of dogs and cats, the clear front-runners for pets owned in America today are fish, birds (parrots), livestock, rabbits, other birds (not parrots), horses, hamsters, guinea pigs, turtles and snakes. Ferrets, gerbils and lizards are also preferred pets, but in smaller numbers.

When I was a young child, one of my dearest friends was a cream-colored hamster named Flower. Flower was never far from my side. She joined me on numerous family vacations (to the dismay of both my grandmothers), visited the beach in the palm of my hand and was my closest confidante. She was also the cause of many sleepless nights as she ran on her wheel or plotted one of her many escapes.

We often treat our pets better than our human families. Surprisingly high numbers of pet owners purchase Christmas gifts for their pets, receive Christmas gifts from their pets, and celebrate pet birthdays with gifts, special meals, cakes, songs, the presence of other pets, photographs and special outings.[1] I, myself, held a cat birthday party for my kitten Bailey's first birthday with four of his siblings in attendance. There were treats and gifts for everyone, and no one got into a fight! Since then, I have held various celebrations for horse birthdays complete with carrot cake. On a recent shopping trip for a Halloween costume, I noticed the mass marketing of costumes for our pets. I seriously considered dressing Kira up as a rock star!

Our pets are often our preferred and favorite companions. The American Animal Hospital Association conducted a survey of 1,019 pet owners to determine the role animals play in our lives. Of the persons surveyed, 57 percent said they would want a pet as their only companion if stranded on a deserted island; 55 percent considered themselves as mom or dad to their pets; and 80 percent selected companionship as the major reason for having a pet.

Recently, on a television program replaying some of David Letterman's Stupid Pet Tricks, a man brought along his singing dog. When David noted he had brought his "dog" the man's reply was, "No, this is my son."

I frequently refer to my pets as my children, and many of my clients refer to their pets in the same fashion. I have even heard the parents of a childless couple refer to the children's pets as their "grandcat," "granddog" or, in my case, "grandhorse." My fiance often complains that when I arrive home at night I head straight to the barn to kiss my horses before I kiss him. Then he has to contend with the "horse slime" on my face!

Pet owners equate their love for their pets on a level equal to or greater than their love for a best friend, child and even a spouse.[2] We share our homes, our beds and our hearts with our pets. Is it any wonder we worry about them as if they were our children?

When leaving for vacation or a business trip, I routinely leave lengthy lists of "baby sitter" instructions for the care of my "kids." I have even gone as far as to put the instructions in a protective plastic sleeve so that I can update them on a regular basis. I call frequently to check on my pets just as any concerned mother would when absent from her children. I have friends who rarely travel as a result of the worry and concern they experience when leaving their pets in the care of a stranger. To combat this concern, there are entrepreneurial pet lovers who have made lucrative careers from pet-sitting services, doggy day care centers, and first-class kennel and boarding operations. In Orlando, Florida, a local establishment called Miss Emily's Bed and Biscuit caters to the booming bed and breakfast industry for pets.

Studies also have reported that pets are good for our health. They can help lower our blood pressure or assist in our recovery from surgery or a heart attack. For some people, our pets are our only resident family member, providing us with love, affection and a reason to get up in the morning. Longevity and pet companionship are frequently interrelated. Many nursing homes have either adopted pets or instituted policies that allow pet companions in recognition of the beneficial impact animals can have on a person's well-being. Several cats live at a retirement center I visit on a regular basis. The residents tell me the cats make a big difference in their outlook on life. A Golden Retriever regularly goes to work at the center with its owner, who is one of the center's employees. This dog is a favorite among the many residents who look forward to his visits.

4

I once read a story about a lady who trained her miniature horse to ride in her minivan so they could visit nursing home residents. She commented on the joy exhibited by the residents in seeing a horse, even a miniature—something they thought they would never see again. I understand there are long-term care insurance companies that provide a premium discount for people who own pets in recognition of the beneficial impact our pets can have on our health.

Many nursing homes and senior centers have implemented Pet Facilitated Therapy programs as well. My sister, Karen, and her beloved Jack Russell terrier, aptly named "Jack," are certified to visit nursing homes. Karen and Jack, as well as the nursing home residents, benefitted from her frequent visits.

Even communities are acknowledging the tremendous value animals and our pets can bring to our lives. The not-for-profit organization, The Harmony Institute, is working with a local Central Florida developer to create a town to be known as Harmony. The town of Harmony will be dedicated to the realization that people live longer, happier and healthier lives when their relationships with animals and their environment are in balance. For more information about The Harmony Institute, you can visit their web site at www.harmonyinstitute.org.

There have been numerous times when one of my cats, dogs or horses has been a source of great comfort to me. In fact, in these days of high stress and long workdays and work weeks, my principal source of real fun and relaxation often is a morning or afternoon horseback ride. Just spending time with my pets can help relieve the stress of life. Each evening as I pull into my driveway, Kira runs at full speed to greet me, no matter where she might be in the yard. Her enthusiastic greeting certainly helps me leave my workday behind.

Some of us spend more money on our pets than we spend on ourselves. I know this is true in my home. I like to tell people the only reason I go to work is to support my pet habit. In 1996, The American Veterinary Medical Association reported the average annual veterinary medical expenditure per household was $186.80 for dogs, $147.19 for cats, $10.95 for birds and $226.26 for horses.[3] This means that as a nation we spend approximately $7.0 billion annually for the veterinary care of our dogs, $3.97 billion each year for our cats, $91.2 million for our birds and $396.3 million for our horses. These astounding numbers are just for veterinary care including physical exams, spay or neuter (as appropriate), vaccinations, emergency care, drugs and medications. They do not include the billions spent annually for grooming, food, toys and other items purchased at retail pet supply stores, from pet supply catalogs or on the Internet.

Unfortunately, the whole truth about how we treat our pets includes brutal cruelty and neglect. Despite our love for our pets, there are some shocking statistics regarding pet ownership. A staggering number of animals die annually as a result of pet overpopulation. The Humane Society of the United States (HSUS) estimates that 4-5 million cats and dogs are euthanized in shelters each year. Even more shocking is the fact that approximately 25 percent are pure-bred or pedigreed animals.

Even if, as pet lovers, we can live with these numbers by acknowledging there are just not enough good homes for all of the animals in need, there is an even more tragic problem. Many animal shelters become cheap sources for animals used in biomedical research and experimentation. Well-meaning individuals place their animals in shelters under the assumption the shelter will find them a good home. Unfortunately, this is not always true. Additionally, thousands of animals are living on the streets, eating out of trash cans, preying on wildlife and becoming victims of highway accidents.

If we view all of God's creatures as "our animals," one legacy we can all leave is the sterilization of our pets to prevent unwanted litters of puppies and kittens. I remember presenting a report in school when I was in fifth grade. I told my classmates that 10,000 unwanted puppies and kittens were born every hour! I have never forgotten the impact those statistics had on my attitude toward our ongoing responsibility to all animals.

Years later, the HSUS reports that a single female dog and her offspring can produce 67,000 puppies in six years. A female cat and her young can produce more than six times that number—a staggering 420,000 kittens—in seven years! There are numerous organizations dedicated to the implementation of low-cost spaying and neutering as well as innovative legislation and mass-media educational programs to build awareness of this ongoing problem. It is a problem for which we all bear the responsibility.

Many of us, however, dedicate our lives to raising our "fur-faced" children in environments where they are well fed and safe, enjoy appropriate and regular veterinary care, and are considered members of our family. This book is for you—to provide guidance, ideas and suggestions for ways to leave an ongoing legacy of your undying love and devotion for your pets. Throughout the book, I will mention a variety of ideas and organizations that have found their way into my heart and thoughts. There are many other ways and many other organizations that will occur to you. Some of the ways we can leave a legacy include:

1) **Make a memorial contribution to the animal care organization of your choice.** The HSUS has developed the Kindred Spirits memorial program specifically for this purpose. A donation to the HSUS through the Kindred Spirits program will allow you to honor the memory of your pet while helping all animals. Upon receipt of your gift, the HSUS will send a card of sympathy (to the person of your choice) acknowledging your donation, and the pet's name will be added to the *Book of Kindred Spirits*, maintained at the HSUS national headquarters. I recently added the names of two of my pets when they died: Bandit, my 14-year-old Sheltie-mix rescued from the Daytona Beach Humane Society; and Beau, my one true love, a 21-year-old Siamese-mix cat purchased for ten dollars when I was in college.

2) **Hold a memorial service in honor of your pet.** This act of love can help grieving family members find closure and offer them a way to explain death to children. Your memorial service can take any form that provides you, your family or a grieving pet owner with an opportunity to say good-bye.

3) **Find a special place for the burial of your pet or your pet's ashes.** There are many businesses today dedicated to providing funeral services and products to assist you in providing a permanent memorial in honor of your beloved pet. You can purchase caskets, urns, headstones or markers to memorialize the passing of your pet. If local regulations or ordinances prohibit burying your pet in your own yard, there are pet cemeteries available for this purpose. Cremation is another option so that the final disposition of your pet's ashes can be at a time and in the special manner you choose. My cat Beau (21) and my dog Bandit (14) were privately cremated with the ashes returned to me so I could plan my own service. My kitten Bailey (2) is buried in my horse pasture.

4) **Create a living memorial.** Consider creating a garden, planting a tree, or introducing some other living reminder of your pet. A name and/or picture marker signifying your pet's life could be placed in the vicinity of your living memorial.

5) **Compose a poem or song or write a story or diary entry remembering your special pet.** Illustrate it with pictures.

This is an idea that does not have to wait for the loss of your pet. I started a diary for my Premarin filly, Sierra, when I adopted her. It continues to grow with stories, pictures and memories of her "childhood." I hope someday to use its entries as the focus of a book for children to educate them about the horrors of the cruelty-based Premarin industry.[i]

6) **Make a memory book or photo collage. Many craft stores can provide the tools and supplies necessary to create a beautiful and permanent memory of your pet.** Find creative ways to incorporate your pet's favorite toys. There are even home party companies that specialize in creating and providing the resources for unique, individualized and creative memory books.

7) **Make a video during your pet's lifetime depicting the different stages of growth, special events or accomplishments.** This video should also include pictures of you enjoying and loving your pet. These lasting memories will be a source of comfort in future years.

8) **Prepare a well-designed, regularly updated estate plan.** Your estate plan should provide for you, your family, your pet and those charitable organizations that can benefit generations of future pets.

There are an unlimited number of ways we can leave a legacy to remember our pet in perpetuity. This book is designed to introduce you to a variety of options, including estate and legacy planning considerations to benefit people as well as their pets. We will consider alternative plans for our pets who survive us, and plans for our future without our pets. Then, we will share some loved poems, stories and thoughts about our favorite pets.

---

1   The American Pet Products Manufacturers Association (APPMA) 2001-2002 National Pet Owners Survey.

2   Ibid.

3   American Veterinary Medical Association, *U.S. Pet Ownership and Demographic Sourcebook* (Center for Information Management, American Veterinary Association, 1997).

4   Premarin is a female hormone replacement therapy created from pregnant mare urine (hence the name). The result of the pregnancy is an unwanted foal. I have seen figures reporting that more than 50,000 unwanted foals are sent to slaughter annually. There are a number of alternative therapies available to women today. Consult with your doctor if you are currently taking Premarin or a related drug for more information about alternative drug therapies.

NOTES

Planning for Your Pet's Future

What to do if something happens to you

Although we would like to believe we will always be present to care for our pets, far too often this is not the case. If, as a result of illness or injury, you must move from your home to an alternate or permanent care facility such as a hospital or nursing home or you become incapacitated or die without addressing the ongoing care of your pet, the outlook for your pet may be grim. There are many sad stories of pets forgotten or overlooked when their owners became ill, had to be hospitalized, went to a nursing home or passed away.

Tragically, pets have run away or have been forgotten in the home of their owner. The horrific events of September 11, 2001, highlighted the thousands of pets with no place to go when their owners were unable to reach them or care for them. To prevent these unnecessary and tragic occurrences, it is imperative to develop a written action plan for your pet in the event you are the victim of an unexpected occurrence or disaster.

13

IDEAS FOR YOUR ACTION PLAN

1) **Identify at least two people—"pet caregivers"—who agree to be responsible for your pet if something happens to you, including incapacity, death or unavailability due to natural disaster.** These trusted individuals should have access to your home, care and feeding instructions for your pet, the name and contact information for your veterinarian, and written instructions for the long-term or permanent care of your pet, including final plans for your pet in the event your pet should die. The individuals you choose can either be short-term, long-term or permanent caregivers depending on the plan you intend to implement for your pet. (Note: I prefer to use the term "caregiver" rather than "caretaker" for obvious reasons.)

2) **Formulate your written action plan to include the following provisions:**

   a. Name, age and medical history of each pet. If you maintain a medical history file for your pet, provide instructions where these documents are stored and can be located. Consider assembling a notebook or 3-ring binder to hold this valuable information. A notebook or binder that allows you to easily add or remove pages will permit you to update your pet's information on a regular basis. Keep this information in a safe but accessible place in your home.

   b. Name, address, phone and other contact information for your veterinarian in the event of an emergency.

Consider an alternate veterinary choice or emergency care facility in the event your regular veterinarian is unavailable.

c. Name, address, phone and other contact information for key family members or friends who can be contacted in the event your pet caregiver is unable or unwilling to provide care services for your pet.

d. Identify the location of your important estate planning and financial documents, including powers of attorney, living trusts, wills, and advance health care directives. These documents should outline your instructions not only to take care of you, but your pets as well.

In our law practice, my partner and I rarely advise our clients to keep this type of documentation in a safe deposit box. Our concern is that the information be easily accessible at any time, day or night, weekday or weekend, and without court order. We also share a philosophy about planning that focuses not just on estate planning in the event of death, but also on short-term and long-term incapacity issues. In our society today, it is not dying too soon but living too long that can provide a number of estate planning challenges. A focus on possible incapacity is as important for your beloved pets as it is for you. As life expectancy increases, we all need to be concerned about the plans we make for ourselves and our loved ones, including our pets.

The instructions you leave for your pets are the equivalent to baby sitter instructions. These are the same type of instructions we would compile and use in the event we were leaving our human children with a baby sitter for the first time. For those of us who have had this experience, it is unlikely we simply handed our child over to a baby sitter without further instruction. Therefore, your written instructions must include every bit of information necessary for a surrogate caregiver to provide adequately for your pet—in all likelihood, you may not be available for further questions or instructions. Keep these instructions in a protective plastic covering or notebook so you can update them easily and regularly.

e. Identify the person or facility that will provide long-term or perpetual care for your pet if you, your family or your selected caregiver is unable or unwilling to provide this care. Great care and consideration should be given to the selection of these individuals and facilities. I have provided a checklist that can help you identify individuals or facilities that may meet your needs. Chapter 6 provides a checklist that can help you make an informed decision about long-term care facilities.

3) **Make and carry in your wallet an emergency Pet Alert Card.** This Pet Alert Card should provide information about your pets, including the names and phone numbers of your emergency caregivers to be immediately

notified in the event you are taken to a nursing home, hospice facility or hospital, or in the event of your death so they can arrange for the immediate care and feeding of your pets. You should also list veterinary numbers, pet names, ages and descriptions, care requirements, as well as their health condition and any special medications they are taking. In addition, be sure your caregivers and veterinarians have updated information on the care and condition of your pets. Your caregivers should know where to locate your more detailed pet-care instructions kept in your home. If you live in an apartment or gated community, make sure your designated caregiver has access to your home in the event of your hospitalization or death so they can care for your pet without delay. You may also want to provide this information to other friends or family members in the event your caregiver is unavailable. Your caregiver and alternates should also know how to access your important estate planning documents, including long-term care instructions for your pets.

4) **Post an "in case of emergency" decal or sticker on the doors and windows of your home identifying the number and types of pets you have along with emergency contact information.** I know of at least one case in which a pet's life could have been saved during a fire if this important information had been available on a door or window. The family dog was locked in an interior bathroom, and fire and rescue professionals had no idea

he was there. These decals can be obtained from a variety of sources or you can make your own.

5) **Include provisions in your estate plan, specifically powers of attorney, wills, living trusts, advance health care directives and other planning documents to detail your wishes with regard to the care and disposition of your pets in the event of your disability or death.** State laws differ as to viability of planning for pets. These various positions will be discussed in greater detail in subsequent chapters.

HAVE YOU DONE PROPER ESTATE PLANNING?

Before we explore the different alternatives and requirements of an effective estate plan that can provide for our pets, let's look at the broader topic of estate planning in general. In other words, let's start at the beginning by asking, "What is proper estate planning?"

Proper estate planning allows you to plan for yourself and your loved ones without giving up control of your affairs. Your estate plan should allow for the possibility of your own disability. It should give "what you have, to whom you want, when you want and the way you want." A comprehensive, well-conceived and custom-designed estate plan should also include fully disclosed and controlled settlement costs for you and for those you love.

TWO PROBLEMS WITH
TRADITIONAL ESTATE PLANNING

The first problem with traditional estate planning is that most estate plans are upside down. In our practice at Hoyt & Bryan, LLC, we view the estate planning process as a pyramid (see Figure 1). The foundation of the pyramid focuses first on you, then on your family. To build a solid foundation, the attorney requires a thorough understanding of your needs, goals, dreams, aspirations and eccentricities—all of the things that make you unique. In the traditional estate planning practice, our experience has been that these conversations are not taking place. Instead, the focus is on documents.

Next, and closely related to you, is a thorough understanding of your family members and your family dynamics—the people or pets you care about and who will someday receive the benefit of your assets. For some people, family includes spouse, children and grandchildren. For others, it could include parents, nieces and nephews, cousins, friends or the community. For some of us, it may only include our pets. For this reason, throughout this book, any reference to "your family" will be presumed to also include all your "children who wear fur coats"—your beloved pet or pets.

You are the expert on matters relating to you and your family. Only you know what it is really like to walk in your shoes—to know what it is like to be your spouse, your

Estate Planning Pyramid

Figure 1

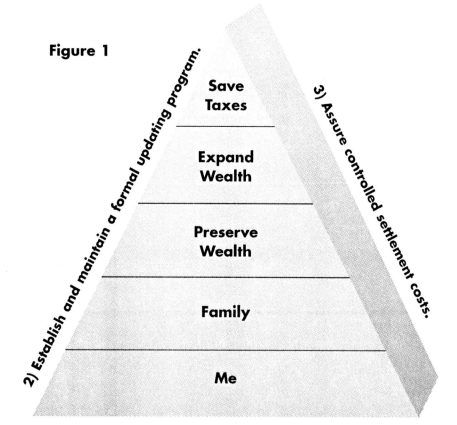

1) Work with a counselling-oriented attorney.

"I want to control my property while alive and well,
plan for me and my loved ones if I become mentally
disabled, and give what I have, to whom I want,
when I want and the way I want—all with fully disclosed
and controlled costs to me and those I love."

20

friend, your relative, your child or your pet. In our practice, my partner and I rely on our clients to teach us about themselves and their family. In turn, we teach them about the law. That way, together we can build an estate plan that works for you and your family.

After the foundation of the pyramid is firmly in place, it is appropriate to discuss wealth (synonymous with assets) and your financial condition. We find that most people first want to protect and preserve the wealth they have, and then they are also interested in enhancing that wealth. In many ways, our role is that of diagnostician. We can review a person's financial situation along with the strategies and tools they have employed to accomplish their goals. In addition, we can help identify those areas or issues that might be considered "spots on an x-ray"—concerns that may require immediate or future consideration.

In this layer of the pyramid, the experts are generally outsiders—those persons who comprise your trusted advisor team, including financial advisors, insurance professionals and certified public accountants. It is important that these professionals be involved in the creation and implementation of your estate plan. Utilizing a team approach to estate planning is just one of the elements required to create an estate plan that works.

The final building block of the pyramid is made up of techniques, strategies and tools designed to save income taxes or estate taxes. This is the stratum of the pyramid where the estate planning and tax lawyers are the experts.

This is also the area where these professionals feel the most comfortable and have the most information. It is for this reason that many traditional estate planning professionals focus on the top of the pyramid rather than the foundation. For my partner and me, the top of the pyramid is like the last piece of a jigsaw puzzle—this is the easiest piece to fit in if all of the proper groundwork has been laid.

When I say that most estate plans are upside down, I mean that most traditional estate plans are built on tax planning goals and objectives instead of family issues, values and ideals. Personal family goals and objectives are relegated to a lower priority instead of being the very foundation of the plan. And we all know what happens when you stand a pyramid on its head! In our firm, we believe that by planning according to the priorities of the pyramid we can better focus on people and family goals and create solutions that will ultimately make the planning easier and more effective.

The second problem with traditional estate planning is that most estate plans just don't work! An estate plan "works" if every expectation the individual had in mind when they began planning is completely met. Of course, it is really the family members who will see and benefit from the result. If you have ever heard someone say after a friend or loved one has passed away, "If (insert name here) only knew what was going on they would be rolling over in their grave"—that's an estate plan that didn't work!

Why is it most estate plans don't work? In our firm, we believe it is because many clients and professional advisors view estate planning as a single transaction. The sentiment generally is "I did my estate plan." Once a person has left the legal professional's office, they assume their estate plan is complete, sometimes never to be reviewed again. In reality, estate planning is a process, never a transaction. As in life, there are constant changes. Therefore, your estate plan must be changing too.

THREE TYPES OF CHANGE AN ESTATE PLAN FACES

The first type of change an estate plan faces is change that directly affects you and your family, both personal and financial. The problems with this type of change arise as a result of your role as expert on yourself and your family. There is no way for your estate planning professionals to learn about these changes unless you tell them. Our experience has been that most people don't communicate regularly with their professional advisors, thereby putting their estate plan in danger of failing. Sometimes, people are discouraged from communicating with their professional advisors because of the actual or perceived cost of communicating changed circumstances. In other words, people tend to communicate with their advisors less when they know there is an invoice attached.

The second type of change an estate plan faces is change to either the tax laws or laws that can affect the personal planning protections provided in your estate plan. An example would include either changes to a federal or state law or statute, or a significant case decision that may affect future planning decisions. In 2001 alone there were two major revisions to the Internal Revenue Code, not to mention numerous significant statutory and case law decisions at the state level.

The third type of change an estate plan faces is change in your attorney's or professional advisor's experience. Many professionals are committed to constantly improving their practices, their knowledge and the quality of their planning. Others continue to practice the same way they always have. Does your attorney have years of cumulative experience or are they still doing things the same old way? In the chapter on Selecting an Estate Planning Attorney, look for guidance on evaluating your attorney's commitment to excellence.

THE ESTATE PLANNING SOLUTION— THE THREE STEP STRATEGY ™

It's not about documents—it's about results! The key to proper estate planning is clear, comprehensive, customized instructions for your own care and that of your loved ones. These instructions can be included in a will, a trust and in several other related documents. We find that most of our clients are best served with a combination of these tools, backed up by the Three Step Strategy™. The Three Step Strategy™ is an approach to estate planning which recognizes that certain processes have to be firmly in place to create estate plans that work!

THE THREE STEPS

Step 1) Work with a Counselling-Oriented Attorney (as opposed to a word processing-oriented attorney). In our practice, we fear that much of what passes for estate planning in this country today is little more than word processing! We don't believe you should pay a licensed professional to fill out forms or to do only word processing. The value of a professional is in their counsel and advice, based on knowledge, wisdom and experience. If word processing is all you want, you might as well do it yourself! But if you want an estate plan that works, seek good counselling. (Note: I've incorporated the old English spelling for "counselling," which denotes an approach that focuses on the role of attorney as advisor and counsellor at law.)

Step 2) Establish and Maintain a Formal Updating Program. We've already noted that an estate plan faces a myriad of changes. First, there is constant change in your personal, family and financial situation. Second, there are inevitable changes in both tax laws and non-tax laws that impact your estate plan. Third, there is (or should be) ongoing change in your attorney's experience and expertise. Your professional advisors should be continually improving their performance and expanding their knowledge through ongoing education and collective experience.

Since everything, except human nature, constantly changes, you cannot expect a plan to accomplish what it was intended to accomplish if it is never updated. The costs of failing to update your plan are typically far greater than the costs of keeping your plan current. The National Network of Estate Planning Attorneys, an organization my partner and I belong to, informally polled its clients and discovered that, on average, people update their estate plans every 19.6 years! This is far too true for many people we know. I know of a number of estate plans in which the failure to update the plan could have resulted in a cost to the individual of 100 percent of his or her estate. Circumstances had changed to the extent that 100 percent of their estate would have gone to unintended beneficiaries.

Step 3) Assure Fully Disclosed and Controlled Settlement Costs after Your Death. The cost of any estate plan has three distinct parts: 1) The part you pay for counselling and design up front (or for word processing)—the cost today; 2) The part you pay for updating (or the potentially larger cost of failing to update)—the cost over time; and 3) The part your loved ones pay after death—the ultimate costs of settlement, administration and distribution. Regardless of the documents chosen (a will or a trust), there are always after-death costs.

Wills are administered through probate; trusts have to be settled or administered. In either case, assets must be transferred to their intended beneficiaries and often a death tax return must be prepared. Be sure you are discussing all three parts of the cost of your estate plan with your attorney before you begin to plan. Understand what all the costs will be in advance, and ask how they can be controlled.

THE IMPORTANCE OF
THE TEAM APPROACH

Creating an estate plan is not difficult, but it does require a commitment on your part as well as the involvement of all your professional advisors: your attorney, your accountant and your financial and insurance advisors. Depending on your plan, it may also require the participation of a planned giving professional for the charitable organization(s) of your choice. If all the professionals are included in the planning, you are far more likely to have an estate plan that works. If not, you may receive conflicting advice that leads to confusion and inaction.

You may have heard the term "analysis paralysis" to describe the confusion and inaction that results when there are too many choices. The most effective approach is to involve all your advisors in your planning, and keep them apprised of steps you are taking. That way, everyone is fully informed and has a chance to offer their particular expertise to the process. A proper estate plan meets your goals and keeps you in control of the process and the results!

OTHER PROBLEMS
WITH ESTATE PLANNING

The Importance of Title

Everything in estate planning comes down to title! Personal planning protections depend on title. Pet protections depend on title. Tax savings depend on title. In other words, you and your family only receive the benefits of your planning if your planning controls your wealth (your assets). Control of your assets and your estate plan comes from and is directly related to asset ownership and title.

There are basically three types of title: *1)* Individual name; *2)* Joint name; and *3)* Contract ownership or beneficiary designation. Individual name property is anything you own in your name alone. Joint name property includes tenancy in common, joint tenancy with rights of survivorship (I call this "He who lives the longest wins") and, in some states, tenancy by the entirety (owned by husband and wife). Contracts include beneficiary designations (such as the beneficiary on insurance policies and retirement plans) and trust ownership (revocable living trusts and irrevocable trusts of all types, including insurance trusts and charitable trusts).

Assets owned in individual name are the only assets that are controlled by a will (or intestacy if there is no will or other estate plan). Jointly owned accounts and beneficiary designations are controlled by operation of law. This means they pass to the surviving owner (if joint tenancy with rights of survivorship or tenancy by the entireties); to your heirs or devisees (if tenants in common); or to the named beneficiary (if a beneficiary designation is elected). ONLY assets owned directly by a trust or in which the named beneficiary is the trust are controlled by the instructions in that trust.

Pitfalls of Jointly Owned Property

- Joint tenancy property can pass to unintended heirs.
- Joint tenancy does not avoid probate, it only delays it.
- There may be unintended gift and estate taxes if joint tenancy is used between non-spouses or with children.
- Joint tenancy property may be subject to your joint tenant's creditors.
- Joint tenancy makes no provisions for estate tax planning.
- Joint tenancy does not allow you to give your property to whom you want, the way you want and when you want.
- Joint tenancy can be problematic in the event of mental disability.
- Joint tenancy will not allow for specific instructions to care for your pets.

Pitfalls of Planning with a Beneficiary Designation

- Designating your beneficiaries on a standard business form "beneficiary designation" often means losing control of a major part of your estate. It does not enable you to leave instructions or provide guidance to your loved ones.

- Often the wrong beneficiary is named in the beneficiary designation.

- A beneficiary designation will not protect your spouse and children from creditors or unscrupulous people.

- Equal distributions from a beneficiary designation can cause unequal results that will not meet your family's special needs.

- Beneficiary designations make no provisions for federal estate tax planning.

- You cannot name your pet as a designated beneficiary.

Pitfalls of a Will

- Wills guarantee probate—which can generate executor or personal representative and attorney fees and cause time delays before your loved ones can receive their inheritance. Complaints about probate generally include statements such as, "It costs too much," "It takes too long" and "It is totally public."

- Wills are public documents recorded in the public records of the local courthouse. They are open to inspection by anyone who wants to know about the contents of your will and your affairs.

- Wills offer no planning or direction for you or your family in the event of your mental disability.

- Wills may be challenged by unhappy relatives.

※ Wills often do not control their maker's life insurance proceeds, retirement benefits or jointly owned property.

※ Wills are often "bare-bones" form documents written in hard-to-understand language. They do not capture the hopes, fears, dreams, values and ambitions of their makers.

※ Wills may not be effective when their makers move to or own property in another state. An ancillary administration may be required for out-of-state property, necessitating additional time, costs and publicity.

※ Under the current law of most states, a pet cannot be named as a beneficiary of your will.

Pitfalls of a Trust

※ Although most living trusts appear to be better than wills, they are about the same as wills if not fully funded because then the assets do not avoid probate. A fully funded trust will own or control all of your assets. Assets not owned or controlled by the trust do not necessarily avoid probate and may require a probate administration.

※ Most living trusts are sterile legal forms that do not contain personalized instructions for loved ones, especially our pets.

※ Trusts only accomplish limited objectives.

※ Under the current law of most states, a pet cannot be named as a beneficiary of your trust.

31

This chapter has focused on the importance of having a well-formulated and documented action plan. We have explored some of the problems with estate planning in general and traditional estate planning specifically. In addition, we have outlined the pitfalls of planning, including the importance of title and the necessity for updating. Also important are the costs associated with planning and understanding that the cost of an estate plan is more than what we might pay for the documents. Remember, estate planning isn't about documents, it's about results!

Estate Planning Options

There are a variety of estate planning options for you and your pets. This chapter will describe alternatives for providing for your pet in the event of your disability as well as your death.

Studies have revealed that somewhere between 12 and 27 percent of pet owners include their pets in their wills.[1] However, as we have already noted, a will does nothing to protect you or your pets in the event of your disability. Therefore, I feel confident that very few people have done anything to provide for their pets in the event of the pet owner's disability, either mental or physical.

It is important to plan not only for the long-term care of your pet if you die, but also for the short-term care of your pet in the event of your incapacity or hospitalization, or during the time between your death and the implementation of your estate plan.

A comprehensive estate plan should include, at a minimum, the following documents:

1) Durable powers of attorney for financial matters.
2) Durable powers of attorney for health matters, sometimes

referred to as advance health care directives or health care powers of attorney. Advance health care directives may also include living wills for end-of-life issues and anatomical gift declarations for at-death donations of organs or tissue.

3) Last will and testament.

4) Trusts (living trusts created during lifetime, testamentary trusts created by a will at the time of death, irrevocable trusts such as insurance or wealth replacement trusts, and charitable trusts).

The key to creating an enduring legacy for your pet is advance preparation, selecting the proper attorney, selecting proper "helpers" and participating in an estate planning process to ensure your estate plan will work. As a general rule, pets cannot inherit your estate, either your property or your money. However, that does not mean there are not legacy planning techniques that can be used to provide for your pet during your disability or in the event of your death.

PLANNING FOR YOUR DISABILITY

During lifetime, it is important to include our pets in our durable powers of attorney (both financial and health care) to authorize payments for care, including, but not necessarily limited to, food, water, veterinary care, grooming, exercise and socialization. (Appendix C includes sample language that may be helpful.)

I have prepared special limited powers of attorney for the sole purpose of authorizing veterinary care while the owner is on vacation or away on business. Important considerations will include where your pet is to reside: at your home as long as you are there, or elsewhere in the event you must be hospitalized or moved to a long-term care facility. Your health care surrogate or health care agent—the trusted individual you have selected and named in your advance health care directives to make your health care decisions—should either be authorized to select an alternate residence for your pet in the event you must be moved from your home or authorized to make provisions for your pet in accordance with your pre-planned written instructions. Consideration should also be given to options that may permit your pet to visit with you during your incapacity, depending on the type of facility in which you may be residing. Today many retirement centers and long-term care facilities permit pets on the premises, as they have acknowledged the beneficial role pets can play in decreasing recovery time and increasing the longevity of our lives. I have had clients tell me their pets were the only thing giving their life purpose and giving them a reason to live.

Failure to make these critical decisions could have tragic results—you return home from an extended hospital or nursing home stay to discover your beloved pet has been given away, has been placed in a shelter, or, worse yet, has died from lack of care or has been euthanized.

PLANNING FOR YOUR DEATH

If a will is used as your primary after-death estate planning tool, it should include a provision that will identify your pre-determined pet caregiver (and at least one alternate) to assume guardianship or ownership of your pet as well as care for your pet. The selection of this individual and their alternates will be critical. Great care must be taken to update your will on a regular basis in the event your designated pet caregiver is no longer willing or able to honor their commitment to you and your pet.

In addition, your will should provide detailed instructions, along with sufficient funds to permit for the ongoing care of your pet in a manner consistent with the level of care provided by you during your lifetime. The person you have selected as your executor or personal representative (along with alternates) should also be given the flexibility, discretion and authority to make alternative care arrangements for your pet in the event your original instructions cannot be honored. Appendix A includes sample language that may be considered for your will.

If a living trust or testamentary trust (a trust created in a will) is used to distribute your assets at death, you may consider—based on your state law—creating a trust known as a "pet trust." The instructions contained in your pet trust would provide a caregiver for your pet and a trustee with authority to administer your trust, and the assets of the trust, for the benefit of your pet and its care, including food, veterinary care and treatment, entertainment and socialization. You should be as specific as possible regarding the quality of care you want your pet to receive along with any payment or reimbursement for expenses to be received by the caregiver. It cannot be over-emphasized that the selection of your caregiver and alternates is going to be critical. I have included sample trust language in Appendix A. Be sure to consult with your legal professional regarding the use of a pet trust in your state.

Living trusts are often preferred over will planning for pets because a living trust takes effect immediately when created. Therefore, it becomes effective during your lifetime, while you are still alive, well and in control of your affairs. With a living trust, there is no delay after disability or death waiting for the appointment of a successor trustee. Your named successor trustee will step into your shoes and take over the day-to-day management of your personal and financial affairs, as well as the care or oversight for the care of your pet.

MONETARY   CONSIDERATIONS

The instructions or language in your trust might provide that your pet be left to a named trustee with directions to deliver custody of your pet to your pre-determined caregiver or alternate. The long-term care of your pet will require that you carefully compute the amount of money that may be necessary to care for your pet and to provide for the expenses, fees or remuneration, if any, for the caregiver and the trustee. Be sure to plan for every possible contingency including: care and board for your pet if your caregiver is temporarily unavailable; emergency care in the event of illness or injury; special care requirements for your pets; and final disposition costs in the event your pet dies.

Many factors may determine the amount of money necessary for the long-term care of your pet, such as the type of pet, the pet's life expectancy, the standard of care you want to provide for your pet, and the need for unanticipated, potentially expensive or extensive medical treatment. I think I do an excellent job of providing for my pets, especially my horses. But when I compare the level of care provided to my pets versus the level of care provided by some of my friends, the care costs of my friends definitely rise to a different level. Some pets may require a special diet or supplements, and these additional care requirements will certainly add to the overall long-term care costs for your pet. Therefore, be sure to take into consideration your unique special care requirements.

The relative size of your estate must be considered in light of your care requirements. If your estate is substantial (more than sufficient to provide for the lifetime care of your pet), you could require that your trustee utilize only the income from your assets. The principal could be retained for unexpected events and emergencies or for the benefit of your alternate or remainder beneficiaries after the care of your pet is complete and your pet has died.

On the other hand, if your estate is modest, you may wish to include language for your trustee that provides discretionary authority permitting your trustee to utilize income first and then principal as may be required for the care of your pet. For some people, the purchase of a life insurance policy naming your trust as the primary beneficiary to provide the assets and liquidity necessary for the ongoing long-term care of your pet would be advised. Consult with an insurance professional before making any life insurance decisions.

If substantial sums of money or assets are left for the benefit of your pet, either by will or by trust, it is possible your heirs or other remainder beneficiaries may attack or contest the provisions of your estate plan. Even if you have no intention or desire to benefit anyone other than your pet, including family members, friends or charities, either at the time of your death or until after your pet has passed away, you should consider all of your estate planning alternatives. It is possible the court could substitute its judgment for your wishes if heirs or remainder beneficiaries successfully challenge your estate plan. In a Pennsylvania court case, the judge reduced the amount of money left in trust to a pet to an amount it considered "reasonable" and sufficient to accomplish the owner's purpose.[2] Another Pennsylvania case reduced the amount left for an animal's care based on the premise the pet owner made an error in determining how much money would be needed to care for his pets.[3] No matter how much money you decide to leave for your pet, the best advice is to make your care calculations carefully.

THE IMPORTANCE
OF WRITTEN INSTRUCTIONS

In order to avoid unnecessary claims by heirs or other beneficiaries asserting that your caregiver is spending an unreasonable amount on your pet, you should provide your caregiver with specific written direction regarding the care of your pets and the associated costs of care. A challenge to your will or trust can be costly to your estate. The cost of defending a challenge to the validity of your estate plan can directly affect your beneficiaries—in this case, your pet. For this reason, you will want to take all necessary precautions to avoid unnecessary litigation. You may consider adding language to your planning regarding alternative dispute resolution such as mediation or arbitration instead of litigation. This is one example of how your detailed "baby sitter" instructions can be valuable in planning for your pet. It is possible to document what you are presently spending on the care of your pet and incorporate that information in your written instructions to your caregiver.

Of course, special consideration needs to be given to unexpected events, emergencies and critical illnesses. One of my friends had a horse that suffered for years with a debilitating form of laminitis (a crippling illness related to the horse's hooves) that increased her veterinary and farrier expenses to a realm some of us may not have been willing or able to endure. Each month, my horse magazines detail extraordinary illnesses and the lengths the owners went to in order to save their beloved horses. Murphy's Law requires we always need to plan for the unexpected—whatever can happen, will. Any other approach is simply wishful thinking, and too much is riding on our decisions.

DURATION OF THE TRUST

Experts recommend that the duration of your pet trust should not be linked to the life of your pet to avoid problems with the rule against perpetuities. (This can be especially important if planning for cats—especially those with nine lives!) The duration of your trust should be measured in terms of a human life unless your state law authorizes pet or animal trusts or has modified or abolished the rule against perpetuities. The rule against perpetuities essentially says that a trust cannot have perpetual existence or an unlimited life; it has to end as some identifiable point in time. In Florida, the rule against perpetuities was recently modified to increase the duration of a trust from 90 years to 360 years for trusts created after December 31, 2000.[i]

MONETARY DISTRIBUTION OPTIONS

There are an unlimited number of ways to provide for the distribution of assets for the benefit of your pet. Here are a few of the alternatives:

Lump Sum

A single lump sum of money in a predetermined amount could be distributed to a trust, a trustee or a caregiver for the benefit of your pet. The dollar amount of this lump sum distribution would be determined based on your calculations for the long-term care of your pet, taking into consideration all contingencies. If desired, you could leave your entire estate for the benefit of your pet if you feel confident the likelihood of a challenge to your estate plan by disappointed heirs or remainder beneficiaries is sufficiently small.

Fixed Sum

A fixed sum of money could be paid by the trustee to the caregiver on a periodic basis (daily, weekly, monthly, quarterly or annually) regardless of the actual expenses incurred by the caregiver for the care of your pet. If the expenses for the care of your pet are less than the fixed distribution amount, the caregiver would enjoy an unexpected benefit for their services. If the pet-care expenses are greater than the fixed distribution amount, your instructions could require the caregiver to personally pay for the additional care costs. An alternative could permit the caregiver to apply to the trustee for additional reimbursement, perhaps based on documented out-of-pocket expenses exceeding the fixed distribution amount. Depending on the size of your estate, this may be a suitable option.

A c t u a l   E x p e n s e s   O n l y

This option would require the caregiver to submit receipts to the trustee for the actual expenses associated with the care of your pet on a periodic predetermined basis. The trustee would review the submitted expenses to ascertain if they are consistent with the level of care specified in your written pet-care instructions. The caregiver would receive reimbursement only if the expenses were approved. Although this option may be consistent with your intent and therefore, reflect only the actual costs of the care of your pet, there will certainly be additional administrative costs to the trustee. There may also be additional effort required on the part of the caregiver to retain and submit receipts in order to receive the required reimbursement.

This option will require a cost-benefit analysis as to the complexity versus the desirability of the additional administrative requirements. a question I might ask is "Does this distribution option provide greater protection or greater complexity?" Only you are in a position to decide.

B o n u s   C o m p e n s a t i o n

There are several theories regarding the payment of bonus compensation. Some pet owners feel reimbursement for expenses only or one of the other compensation methods set out in this chapter are sufficient without additional bonus compensation. Others believe the caregiver will do a better job and have a greater sense of loyalty, duty and responsibility if the caregiver is receiving incentive com-

pensation contingent on providing the pet with the specified level of care. If desired, bonus compensation could be
paid on any periodic basis you feel comfortable with—
monthly, quarterly, semi-annually, yearly—or a single
bonus amount paid at the completion of care, generally at
the death of your pet.

Outright Gift of Pet and Assets

This option contemplates that your pet, along with a reasonable lump-sum distribution of cash or assets for the
lifetime care of your pet, will be distributed to the caregiver, outright and free of trust. Therefore, there is no ongoing
administration or oversight responsibility required by the
trustee. However, to provide greater protection for your
pet, the payment of this outright gift could be conditioned
on the caregiver taking proper care of your pet.

  This option is simpler than some of the other options
shared above, but may also be less reliable, and perhaps,
should only be considered if your estate is relatively small.
In the absence of a trustee or animal care panel (described
later) to provide oversight and administration, there may
be an increased likelihood that your instructions for the
ongoing care of your pet will not be carried out in strict
compliance with your wishes and desires.

  If you select this option and elect to make an outright
gift of your pet along with a lump-sum distribution of
money, you should consider whether the caregiver must
actually care for your pet in order to receive the distribution

(a condition precedent) or whether the caregiver will receive the gift regardless of whether the caregiver cares for your pet or not (a condition subsequent).[5] These are lawyer terms, but essentially boil down to conditions that determine if the caregiver will, in fact, receive the intended gift. If you elect a condition precedent, the caregiver receives the distribution of assets only if the caregiver actually cares for your pet. Therefore, if your pet dies before you do, the named caregiver will never receive or benefit from the gift. This option requires that you specifically provide for an alternate disposition of the cash gift if your pet dies before you do. Alternatively, you can specify a condition subsequent. In this case, the caregiver will be guaranteed to receive the gift and will only fail to receive the gift if the caregiver does not provide proper care for your pet.

In our practice, it's been suggested that my partner and I ask "What if" questions too often. Our concern, of course, is to plan for the unexpected—to avoid Murphy's Law. We strongly believe it is the one thing we fail to ask about and to plan for that is bound to happen. "What if" questions and contingency plans are the best way to ensure that you have created an estate plan that works.

REMAINDER BENEFICIARIES

After the lifetime care of your pet is complete and your pet has passed away, it is important to clearly designate a remainder or alternate beneficiary. The alternate beneficiary may be the caregiver or another beneficiary (possibly an animal-centered charity) to receive the balance of the trust property. You should carefully consider all of your alternatives in planning for your pet and the possible impact it could have on surviving family members, the caregiver, the trustee and, ultimately, the remainder beneficiary or beneficiaries. It would be unwise to create a situation that could place your pet in peril because of the unkindness or greed of any potential remainder or alternate beneficiaries. If the remainder beneficiary's inheritance is solely dependent on the passing of your pet, it is not outside the realm of possibility that grave harm could come to your pet.

CLEARLY IDENTIFY YOUR PET

You should clearly identify the pet you intend to receive care under the terms of your trust in order to prevent an unscrupulous trustee or caregiver from replacing a deceased, lost or stolen pet with a substitute. Many breeds have individuals that look remarkably alike. To the untrained eye, one Golden Retriever, Rottweiler, Siamese or Persian is the same as another. In fact, I just recently confused the identity of my friend's horse for another despite the fact I have been around both horses for years. Consider your pet's individual identifying marks, including coloring, spots, scars or any other unique characteristics. Tattoos, microchip technology or DNA samples could be considered for the purpose of clearly distinguishing your pet from a substitute.

Both of my Mustangs display freeze brands (similar to a tattoo) and my puppy, Kira, came from her rescue organization with a microchip embedded under her fur. Both the freeze brands and the microchip would be invaluable in identifying my pets in the event they were lost or stolen.

Consider the following—"[A] trust was established for a black cat to be cared for by its deceased owner's maid. Inconsistencies in the reported age of the pet tipped off authorities to [the] fact that the maid was on her third black cat, the original long since having died."[6] This is not an isolated incident. Make sure your pet can be easily identified.

PERIODIC PET INSPECTIONS

Consider leaving instructions that require your trustee or an animal care panel (see below) to make regular periodic inspections of your pet. The animal care panel could be invaluable in providing the trustee or other named individuals with information related to your pet's ongoing care and condition. Other options include requiring a periodic statement to your trustee or animal care panel from your pet's regular veterinarian attesting to the overall condition of your pet.

In the Bureau of Land Management's Wild Horse and Burro Adoption Program, the adopter acts only as a foster home for the first year. The prospective owner does not receive a certificate of title until the year has elapsed and proof from a licensed veterinarian as to the condition of the horse has been submitted and verified. There can be significant penalties, including fines and incarceration, if the horse is not properly cared for. The day I received my certificates of title for Reno and Tahoe was one of my best days ever. For me, they are adoption certificates—proof that I am a suitable wild horse "mother." My certificates are framed and proudly displayed in my home along with pictures of Reno and Tahoe.

ANIMAL CARE PANEL

Consider creating an animal care panel for on going care and other decisions related to your pet. Your animal care panel could consist of specific individuals charged with the responsibility of making on going care, critical care and other important decisions related to the needs of your pet. This animal care panel, in addition to your selected caregiver, could include concerned family members, trusted friends, veterinarians or other professionals. Your animal care panel could be extremely beneficial in the event your trustee or selected caregiver requires assistance in making long-term health care, critical care or euthanasia-related decisions for your pet, or in the event your pet needs to be moved to an alternate home or perpetual care facility.

I assisted one of my friends in developing an animal care panel for her horses to provide guidance to her daughter, the designated caregiver, in making difficult or long-term health care-related decisions. Panel members could serve unlimited terms or provisions could be included to replace or re-evaluate panel membership on a periodic basis. Consider how alternate panel members will be selected if one or more panel members are unable or unwilling to serve on your animal care panel.

INSTRUCTIONS FOR WHEN YOUR PET DIES

Include instructions for your pet in the event your pet dies. You may want to have your pet cremated with the "cremains" distributed according to your direction, placed in an urn or buried in a special place or in a pet cemetery. However, you may not want to have your pet cremated and instead would prefer to have your pet buried, either in a special place or in a pet cemetery. If you choose burial, there are a number of options for burial containers, as well as costs. The cost for pet burial can range from approximately $100 to more than $1,000. Pet cremations, however, are significantly less expensive. If you choose a pet cemetery, choose carefully. A recently reported case in Florida of a pet cemetery that was being sold resulted in extreme emotional distress for the families whose beloved pets were buried there. Use the checklist in Chapter 6 provided for evaluating a long-term care facility as a guide in selecting a pet cemetery as well. In addition, there is a lot of good information available on the Internet.

There are a number of individuals and organizations that will prepare or provide estate planning documents for the purpose of making lifetime or testamentary bequests for your pets. This is not an area for amateurs or do-it-your-selfers (engineers take note!). Choose a licensed legal professional who is sensitive to your desire to include lega-cy planning for your pet as part of your estate plan and can provide you with information, including the pros and cons of doing legacy pet planning in your particular state. For a list of estate planning attorneys who are members of the National Network of Estate Planning Attorneys, visit www.netplanning.com on the Internet.

TRUSTEE, ADMINISTRATOR, EXECUTOR OR PERSONAL REPRESENTATIVE SELECTION

It is crucial that you select a trusted individual, certified public accountant, bank or trust organization or other licensed fiduciary to administer the assets you have left for the benefit of your pet. These are the people or organiza-tions that will have the responsibility for the administration of your estate, in the event of either your disability or death. They will be in charge of estate administration func-tions such as identifying and gathering the trust or estate assets, paying your bills, identifying and paying your valid creditors, paying your final expenses and thereafter, caring for or overseeing the lifetime care of your pet, and then distributing the balance of your assets to your named beneficiaries. It is imperative, for every selection you make, to also select alternates who can act in the event the first person or organization you have selected is either unwilling or unable to serve for any reason. It is important to note that the person or organization you select as trustee, administrator, executor or personal representative to administer your estate is not necessarily the same person or organization you will choose as the caregiver for your pet. These are two entirely different functions with vastly different responsibilities and areas of expertise. Your trustee, executor or personal representative may be authorized to make the financial investments and distribution decisions for your estate while your caregiver may be charged solely with the day-to-day care responsibilities for your pet. Both roles are vitally important and each should be chosen with the unique requirements of the role in mind.

Many people choose family members or friends to act as the trustee, executor or personal representative of their estates. In some cases, this decision is fine; in other instances, questionable. It is never wise to choose a family member because of the perception that it will be less expensive. Often, you get what you pay for. With regard to the investment of assets, a difference of just one percent in the annual rate of return can often more than justify the cost of a professional trustee or administrator.

Further, the financial cost of employing a professional trustee or administrator could be considerably less than the emotional cost experienced by family members when burdened with this type of responsibility. Few family members are uniquely qualified to provide the long-term administrative functions required of a fiduciary. Those persons we have spoken to who have served in trustee and/or administrator roles are not anxious to volunteer again. The role of fiduciary is a job with significant responsibility (and potential liability). It is not a popularity contest. Therefore, the job may be best left to a professional.

If it is important to have family members involved in the administrative functions, consider naming the family member and professional as co-trustees. Key qualifications to consider when selecting a trustee, administrator, executor or personal representative, whether individual or corporate, are

- Experience in administering estates and investing assets, dealing with creditors and preparing income tax and estate tax returns for individuals and trusts.
- Organizational skill.
- Attention to detail.
- Scrupulous honesty and integrity.
- Good judgment and common sense.
- Discipline.

In some instances, you may not be able to find all of the qualities you desire in a single individual or organization. In those cases, you may consider naming co-trustees, co-executors or co-personal representatives. Remember to weigh the protections provided versus the complexity of administration when naming multiple individuals or organizations.

There is a growing number of organizations dedicated to the administration of estates that name pets as primary beneficiaries. The organization's primary function is to administer and invest the estate or trust assets; regulate the activities of the caregiver; receive reports from your animal care panel, if any; ensure your instructions are followed during your pet's lifetime; and, ultimately, make final distributions according to your instructions when the trust purpose is complete.

ALTERNATIVES TO INDIVIDUAL CAREGIVERS

Today, there are numerous organizations dedicated to the short-term, long-term or perpetual care of pets. They can be found in your area by researching the yellow pages, contacting your veterinarian or local humane society, contacting your local or nearby veterinary school, or utilizing the resources of the Internet. I have researched a number of them on the Internet, something you can do also. I quickly located a dozen or more possible caregiver candidates. You can also contact The Humane Society of the United States for more information about perpetual care facilities.

Your choice of caregiver will be one of the most critical decisions you make. You should feel absolutely comfortable that the person or organization you choose is always going to have your pet's best interests in mind. This topic is discussed in more detail in Chapter 6—Animal Care Organizations.

FAMOUS PEOPLE AND THEIR PETS

Many famous people have been reported to have provisions in their estate plans for their pets. They serve as role models, emphasizing the need for comprehensive estate plans that include their pets. It isn't money, but concern, that dictates the need for a legacy plan for our pets. One interesting example is the will of tobacco heiress Doris Duke, who died in 1993. She is reported to have left $100,000 to her dog, Minnie.[7]

---

1 Gerry W. Beyer, Esquire, "Estate Planning for Pets," *Probate and Property* (July-August 2001): 6, citing Carey and Marcy E. Mullins, "USA Snapshots—Man's Best Friend?," *USA Today*, Dec. 2, 1999, at 1B (12%), Elys A. McLean, "USA Snapshots—Fat Cats—and Dogs," *USA Today*, June 18, 1993, at 1D (27%).

2 Ibid., 9, citing *Templeton Estate*, 4 Fiduciary 2d 172, 175 (Pa. Orphans' Ct. 1984) (applying "inherent power to reduce the amount involved...to an amount which is sufficient to accomplish [the owner's] purpose").

3 Ibid., 9 citing *Lyon Estate*, 67 Pa. D. & C. 2d 474, 482-83 (Orphans' Ct. 1974)(reducing the amount left for the animal's care based on the supposition that the owner mistook how much money would be needed to care for the animals). Cf. Unif. Prob. Code section 2-907(c)(6)(1993)(authorizing the court to reduce amount if it "substantially exceeds the amount required" to care for the animal).

4 See Florida Statute 689.225.

5 Gerry W. Beyer, Esquire, "Estate Planning for Pets," *Probate and Property* (July-August 2001); 11.

6 Ibid., 11, citing Torri Still, "This Attorney is for the Birds," *Recorder* (San Francisco), Mar. 22, 1999.

7 Ibid., citing Walter Scott, *Personality Parade*, Parade Mag., Sept. 11, 1994 at 2; In re Estate of Duke, No. 4440/93, slip op. (NY Sur. Ct. NY County July 31, 1997).

C H A P T E R 4

Estate Planning and Pets

In a recent article, "Estate Planning for Pets," *Probate & Property* (July/August 2001), the author, Gerry W. Beyer, Esquire, discussed the issues related to planning for our pets. Mr. Beyer's article reports that the idea of planning for our pets is nothing new. In England, the common law courts have long looked favorably on gifts to support specific animals.[1] Unfortunately, the English custom of providing for our pets did not, until recently, make its way to America and the American court system.

Today, some American courts and legislatures are embracing the concept of permitting testamentary (at death) gifts to support our pets. One of the reasons is that many states have abolished the rule against perpetuities or have made significant revisions to the rule. Traditionally, the rule against perpetuities has been a stumbling block to providing for our pets.

In non-lawyer terms, the rule against perpetuities says that a trust cannot have a perpetual existence, but must end at some finite time in the future. Historically, the rule against perpetuities measured the "life" of a trust in terms of a human life. This concept has been problematic for trusts that name non-human beneficiaries, such as our pets.

Another bonus to testamentary gift-giving to our pets in America is the recent addition of a new section to the Uniform Probate Code that validates a "trust for the care of a designated domestic or pet animal and the animal's off-spring."[2] States are starting to recognize the desire of individuals to have a valid and enforceable means to include their pets as an integral part of their estate plans.

Attempted testamentary gifts for the benefit of our pets have historically failed for two primary reasons:

1) **The gift violates the rule against perpetuities.** As mentioned above, this is the rule that requires a trust to have a finite or definite life, generally measured in terms of a human lifespan. Generally, where the measuring life for a trust is an animal rather than a human, the rule against perpetuities is violated and, therefore, the bequest will fail.

In Florida, the rule against perpetuities has been amended to permit a trust to exist for a time period not to exceed 360 years. A number of other states, like Alaska and South Dakota, have abolished the rule against perpetuities completely. There are not many lawyers who will mourn the loss of the rule. In *Lucas v. Hamm* (1961), a California lawyer was excused from a charge of professional negligence due to his misunderstanding of the rule! The rule against perpetuities is complex and, as many states have decided, unnecessary.

2) **The gift is deemed to be only an honorary trust.** An "honorary trust" is defined by *Black's Law Dictionary*, 6th Edition, as "a trust for specific non-charitable purposes where there is no definite ascertainable beneficiary and hence unenforceable in the absence of statute." Honorary trusts have traditionally failed because they lacked a human or legal entity as a beneficiary with sufficient legal standing to enforce the terms of the trust. It is legal standing which provides the beneficiary with the elements necessary to bring a lawsuit and enforce their rights. In the animal rights community, this lack of standing for animals has long been a significant issue.

In his article, Mr. Beyer suggests that the most predictable and reliable method to provide for a pet is for the owner to create an enforceable *inter vivos* (during life) trust (also known as a living trust) or testamentary (after death) trust in favor of a human beneficiary (in our context, generally, the caregiver), and then require the trustee to make distributions to the caregiver to sufficiently provide for the pet's long-term expenses. The payment to the caregiver could require proof that the caregiver is taking proper care of your pet. This solution avoids the two traditional problems with testamentary gifts that benefit pets.

First, the actual beneficiary, the caregiver, is a human and, therefore, has sufficient legal standing to enforce the terms and provisions of the trust. Second, there is a human measuring life to combat the rule against perpetuities problem. Even if you live in a state that validates and enforces animal or pet trusts, a conditional gift in trust to the caregiver may provide more flexibility and a greater likelihood your intent will be carried out.[3]

Another author, J. Alan Jensen, Esquire, states that while over two-thirds of pet owners report they treat their animals as members of their family, the laws of most states do not see it the same way after the owner's death.[4] In an estate plan, a person can provide, either by will or trust, for every member of their family except for those family members who wear fur coats—our pets. Unfortunately, most states do not recognize our pets as family members. Most state laws still consider our pets to be items of personal property. Legally, one piece of personal property cannot hold title to another piece of personal property. A desk cannot own a chair. Using this logic, a pet, if considered by law to be personal property, cannot be a beneficiary of either a will or a trust.

In addition, the Internal Revenue Code does not currently recognize a trust whose beneficiary is an animal and, further, does not permit an income tax or estate tax deduction for gifts to a charitable remainder trust when the non-charitable trust distributions are solely for the benefit of an animal.[5] However, there is a bill currently pending in Congress, known as the Morgan Bill, that, if enacted, would amend section 664 of the Internal Revenue Code to permit the creation of a "charitable remainder pet trust." This charitable remainder pet trust would be recognized by the Internal Revenue Service and permit both income tax and estate tax deductions for gifts to benefit pets as well as charities.

The response of our state court systems to a pet owner's attempts to leave a bequest to their pet has varied. In some cases, the gift has been voided and the assets passed to the remainder or residual beneficiaries, if any. Other courts have searched for more creative ways to implement the decedent's wishes, including looking the other way.[6] In 1923, the Kentucky Supreme Court, in the first U.S. case to address the issue, upheld the validity of a bequest to a trust for a benefit of a pet, finding that the gift for the care of a specific animal was a "humane purpose" and, therefore, effective under a Kentucky statute that validated any gift that had a humane purpose.[7]

In cases where courts have deemed a pet trust to be a honorary trust and therefore technically unenforceable, the beneficiary (caregiver) has been permitted to voluntarily carry out the terms of the trust. In these cases, the court has avoided the rule against perpetuities problem by limiting the duration of the honorary trust to 21 years or by determining that the lifespan of the animal beneficiary would not exceed 21 years.[8] This limitation could be potentially problematic or even devastating if the actual lifespan of the animal did, in fact, exceed 21 years, as is often the case with horses, birds, turtles and other animals.

Other courts have carried out the wishes of the deceased pet owner by finding the pet trust language to be precatory (another lawyer word). In non-lawyer English, precatory is defined as "a recommendation, advice or the expression of a wish, but not a positive command or direction"[9] and is, therefore, non-binding on the beneficiary (caregiver). This result prevents the gift from failing, but the beneficiary (caregiver) remains free to voluntarily use the property for the care of the decedent's animals.[10]

In an attempt to overcome or discourage family members or other beneficiaries from challenges to the provisions of a will or trust, some estate planning experts have suggested the use of an *in terrorem* clause. An *in terrorem* provision provides that if there is a challenge to the will or trust the beneficiary/challenger may run the risk of being disinherited. Not all states, however, recognize *in terrorem* clauses. In Florida, an *in terrorem* clause will not be enforced.[11]

As a result of the inconsistencies in our state laws and the unwillingness of some courts to recognize testamentary gifts in favor of our pets, Americans must often rely on the hearts, helping hands and good intentions of our family, friends, caregivers and animal protection organizations for the ongoing care of our "children who wear fur coats."

Some states are beginning to recognize the validity of trust planning for the benefit of our pets. Many of the state statutes track the language of Section 2-907 of the Uniform Probate Code, as amended in 1993. The Uniform Probate Code Section 2-907 has been characterized by its writers as an "optional provision for validating and limiting the duration of so-called honorary trusts and trusts for pets."

UPC Section 2-907 states, in pertinent part:

a. [Honorary Trust] Subject to subsection (c), if (i) a trust is a trust for a specific lawful noncharitable purpose or for lawful noncharitable purposes to be selected by the trustee and (ii) there is no definite or definitely ascertainable beneficiary designated, the trust may be performed by the trustee for twenty-one years but no longer, whether or not the terms of the trust contemplate a longer duration.

b. [Pet Trust] Subject to this subsection and subsection (c), a trust for the care of a designated domestic or pet animal is valid. The trust terminates when no living animal is covered by the trust. A governing instrument must be liberally construed to bring the transfer within this subsection, to presume against the merely precatory or honorary nature of the disposition, and to carry out the general intent of the transferor. Extrinsic evidence is admissible in determining the transferor's intent.

c. [Additional Provisions Applicable to Both Honorary Trusts and Pet Trusts] In addition to the provisions of subsection (a) and (b), a trust covered by either of those subsections is subject to the following provisions:....6. A court may reduce the amount of property transferred, if it determines that the amount substantially exceeds the amount required for the intended use. The amount of the reduction, if any, passes as unexpended trust property...7. If a trustee is not designated or a designated trustee is not willing or able to serve, a court shall name a trustee. A court may order the transfer of the property to another trustee, if required to assure that the intended use is carried out and if a successor trustee is not designated in the trust instrument or if a designated successor trustee does not agree to serve or is unable to serve; a court may also make other orders and determinations as are advisable to carry out the intent of the transferor...

Listed below are some of the states that recognize pet trusts and/or testamentary gifts to pets. This list is by no means exhaustive and state laws are always subject to change. Be sure to consult with your estate planning attorney for more information about your state and its unique requirements. Some states are exceedingly more pet friendly than others.

Alaska – Alaska Statute 13.12.907, www.legis.state.ak.us. Alaska recognizes pet trusts as valid.

Arizona – Ariz. Rev. Stat. Ann. 14-2907, www.azleg.state.az.us. Arizona has validated pet trusts.

California – Cal. Prob. Code Section 15212, www.leginfo.ca.gov/statute.html. California permits trusts for pets but does not recognize them as enforceable trusts.

Colorado – Colo. Rev. Stat. Ann. Section 15-11-901. Colorado's statutes can be located on the Internet at www.intellinetus.com. Colorado enforces pet trusts.

Iowa – Code of Iowa 633.2105, www.legis.state.ia.us. Iowa has recognized pet trusts as valid.

Michigan – Mich. Comp. Laws. Ann. Section 700-2722, www.michiganlegislature.org/law/. Michigan accords pet trusts full force and effect.

Missouri – Mo. Ann. Stat. Section 456.055, www.moga.state.mo.us. Missouri's statute is similar to the California statute regarding pet trusts.

Montana – Mont. Code. Ann. Section 72-2-1017, http://data.opi.state.mt.us/bills. Modeled after Alaska and Arizona, Montana validates pets trusts.

New Mexico – N.M. Stat. Ann. Section 45-2-907, www.legislstate.nm.us/. New Mexico's statute recognizes pet trusts as valid.

New York – Est. Powers & Trusts Section 7-6.1, www.assembly.state.ny.us/leg/. New York's statute make pets trusts fully enforceable.

North Carolina – N.C. Gen. Stat. Section 36A-147 , www.ncga.state.nc.us/Statutes/. North Carolina recognizes the creation of trusts for pets.

Oregon – Oregon Statute Chapter 636, passed in 2001, www.leg.state.or.us. At present, the Oregon statute may go the farthest to protect our children who wear fur coats. The statute specifically makes provisions for persons to take immediate care and custody of a decedent's pet along with reimbursement for costs.

Tennessee – Tenn. Stat. 35-500-118, www.michie.com/. Tennessee, like California, has an honorary trust statute but does not enforce pet trusts.

Utah – Utah. Code. Ann. Section 75-2-1001, www.le.state.ut.us. Utah's statute is similar to many other state statutes regarding honorary trusts and trusts for pets.

Wisconsin – Wis. Statutes Section 701.11, www.legis.state.wi.us/rsb/stats.html. Wisconsin's statute does not specifically refer to pets but permits a trustee to apply the property of a trust to purposes that are not capricious (example: characterized by or subject to whim; impulsive or unpredictable).

Clearly a number of state legislatures are making proactive decisions through the enactment of statutes to allow for pet trusts and/or testamentary gifts to care for our pets. Perhaps one day all of our states will provide an enforceable means of protection for our "children who wear fur coats."

FEDERAL OBSTACLES

Despite the fact that some states are willing to recognize the validity of pet trusts, the Internal Revenue Service still refuses to recognize a pet trust. This may change if the Morgan Bill, currently pending, is passed. However, for now there is no estate tax or income tax deduction allowed under Internal Revenue Code (IRC) Sections, 170, 664,

2055(a) and 2055(e)(2) for the bequest of a remainder interest to a charity if the lifetime income beneficiary is reserved for the care of a pet.[13]

The Internal Revenue Service explains its adverse position regarding pet trusts by referring to the definition of "trust" and "beneficiary."[14] The term "trust" as used in the Internal Revenue Code refers to an *inter vivos* (during life) or testamentary (after death) transfer of property to a trustee on behalf of a beneficiary.[15] Internal Revenue Code section 643(c) defines "beneficiary" to include "heirs, legatees, and devisees." All of these are persons, and, as defined by Internal Revenue Code section 7701(a)(1), "means and includes an individual, a trust, estate, partnership, association, company, or corporation." The result is that a pet or animal does not fit within the Internal Revenue Code's definition of person; therefore, our pets cannot be trust beneficiaries. When a trust lacks a beneficiary, that trust is deemed invalid and unenforceable.

The Internal Revenue Service does, however, conclude that a pet trust "should nonetheless be classified as a trust for tax purposes under Section 641" whenever such a trust is not invalid under applicable state law.[16] Therefore, pursuant to Section 641 of the Internal Revenue Code, the income of a pet trust would be taxable. To do otherwise, the ruling explains, would be to ignore the effect of local law and to allow the trust's income to escape taxation altogether.[17]

Our state and federal governments as a whole have not reached consensus regarding the use and implementation of testamentary gifts for the benefit of our pets. The challenge exists for each of us who care about our pets to work proactively within our country, our states and our communities to support and encourage our leaders to introduce additional pet-friendly legislation.

---

1 Gerry W. Beyer, Esquire, "Estate Planning for Pets," *Probate and Property* (July-August 2001): 7.

2 Ibid., citing Unif. Prob. Code s 2-907, cmt. (1990).

3 Ibid., 8.

4 J. Alan Jensen, Esquire, see www.weiss-law.com/Pet_Tricks.htm.

5 Ibid.

6 Ibid.

7 Ibid., citing <u>Willet v. Willet</u>, 247 S.W. 739 (Ky.1923).

8 Ibid.

9 *Black's Law Dictionary*, 6th Edition.

10 J. Alan Jensen, Esquire, see www.weiss-law.com/Pet_Tricks.htm.

11 Florida Statutes 737.207 (as to trusts), 732.517 (as to wills).

12 J. Alan Jensen, Esquire, see www.weiss-law.com/Pet_Tricks.htm. Portions of this information have been revised or updated with additional research.

13 Ibid.

14 See also Rev. Rul. 76-486, 1976-2 C.B. 192.

15 See Treas. Reg. Section 301.7701-4(a).

16 See Rev. Rul. 76-486.

17 J. Alan Jensen, Esquire, see www.weiss-law.com/Pet_Tricks.htm, citing Rev. Rul. 76-486, 1976-2 C.B. 192.

Gerry W. Beyer may be contacted at: School of Law, St. Mary's University
One Camino Santa Maria
San Antonio, Texas 78228-8603
e-mail: gwb@ProfessorBeyer.com
web site: http://www.ProfessorBeyer.com

Charitable Giving Techniques

People give money and property to charity for a number of reasons. The most common reasons given are

- To help society by funding a worthy cause.
- To enjoy the income tax and estate tax benefits derived from charitable giving.

LIFETIME GIFTS

A donor (the person making the gift) can make lifetime gifts of cash or property to the charity or charities of their choice. One lifetime gift choice is appreciated securities so the donor may avoid the payment of capital gains tax. Given the option, appreciated securities or other appreciated assets should be given as charitable gifts before cash gifts. The donor is entitled to an income tax deduction for outright gifts made during lifetime. The overall income tax effect will depend on the individual donor and their financial circumstances. Gifts to charity through the use of a trust, like a charitable remainder trust, can help reduce the donor's taxable estate not only by the present fair market value of the gift but also by the value of the potential growth of the gift asset over time (appreciation).

TESTAMENTARY GIFTS

Gifts can also be made to charity at the time of death. These are referred to as testamentary gifts. Testamentary gifts can be made in a will or in a trust. Many of the charitable trust techniques discussed in this chapter can be created either in lifetime or testamentary trusts. The choice is up to you, the donor, depending on your personal lifetime income and taxation goals.

CHARITABLE TRUSTS IN GENERAL

There are a number of types of charitable trusts. The most common are charitable remainder trusts of which there are several varieties, and charitable lead trusts. Charitable trusts are often referred to as "split interest gifts" because the gift is shared by two different parties: one that receives the lifetime income stream and one that receives the remainder interest (the amount left over after the income stream has been paid). Essentially, a charitable trust is an irrevocable trust created by a donor during lifetime or at death by testamentary bequest for the purpose of providing a stream of income to a named beneficiary for a period of time, and thereafter the balance of the trusts assets are distributed to a named beneficiary.

The identification of the named beneficiaries for either the income stream or the remainder interest is going to depend on the type of charitable trust created, either a charitable remainder trust or a charitable lead trust. In a charitable remainder trust, the income beneficiary is typically the donor, their spouse or other family members, and the remainder beneficiary is a qualifying 501(c)(3) charity. In a charitable lead trust, the income beneficiary is typically the 501(c)(3) qualifying charity, and the remainder beneficiary is the spouse or family members of the donor.

Charitable trusts provide both income tax and estate tax incentives for the donor. The donor is permitted to take a current income tax deduction for the charitable gift as well as an estate tax deduction at the time of death. It is important to note that the income tax and estate tax are two distinctly different taxes. The value of the income tax and estate tax deductions are determined based on the size of the gift (its fair market value), the present value of the stream of income, and the present value of the remainder interest gift.

CHARITABLE REMAINDER TRUSTS

A charitable remainder trust (sometimes referred to as a CRT) is designed to benefit two different parties. The two parties are the individual(s) receiving the income from the trust and the chosen charity or charities designated to receive the balance or remainder of the trust assets.

A charitable remainder trust is a special type of irrevocable trust that pays income to the donor and/or to the donor's family members for their lifetimes or for a specified term of years. After the income period of the trust ends, the assets remaining in the trust are distributed by the trustee to the selected qualified charity or charities. To be a qualified charity, the charity must be recognized by the Internal Revenue Service as a 501(c)(3) charity. The donor has flexibility in determining what the income distributions will be, who will receive the income from the trust, and what charity or charities will receive the assets when the trust ends. A charitable remainder trust can achieve several significant financial and tax goals, including:

- Avoiding capital gains taxes on the value of the appreciated assets contributed to the trust.
- An increased stream of income over the lifetime of the donor or other family members.
- An income tax deduction to the donor during life.

TYPES OF CHARITABLE REMAINDER TRUSTS

There are a number of types of charitable remainder trusts. The most common are charitable remainder annuity trusts and charitable remainder unitrusts.

Charitable Remainder Annuity Trust

A charitable remainder annuity trust (sometimes referred to as a CRAT) is an irrevocable trust that pays a fixed dollar amount each year to a named beneficiary, such as the donor of the trust assets, their spouse, their children or others. For example, if $100,000 is donated to a six percent charitable remainder annuity trust, the annual income stream would be $6,000. After the death of the income beneficiaries, or at the end of a predetermined number of years, the remaining trust assets are distributed by the trustee to the charity or charities named by the donor in the trust.

Once the charitable remainder annuity trust is created and the income stream determined, no new additional contributions are allowed. A new trust must be established for additional contributions.

The charitable income tax deduction the donor receives is based on the present value of the charity's right to receive the trust assets at some time in the future. A number of factors determine this value:

- The estimated length of time the charity has to wait for its remainder distribution. This length of time is a term of years established by the donor, as limited by the law; the donor's lifetime; or the lifetime of another person.
- The percentage rate payable to the income beneficiaries each year and how frequently the income is paid (annually, quarterly, monthly, etc.).
- The current rate of return on investments as determined by the applicable federal (midterm) rates (AFR). This rate changes on a monthly basis.

If the income from the charitable remainder annuity trust is paid to someone other than the donor or the donor's spouse, it may be subject to federal gift taxation. If certain requirements are met, however, the income gift can qualify for the annual gift tax exclusion currently limited to $10,000 per beneficiary. The gift tax exclusion is indexed for inflation and is expected to increase to $11,000 on January 1, 2002. The unlimited marital deduction usually eliminates any gift tax on payments to the donor's spouse.[1]

For federal estate tax purposes, the value of the remainder interest passing to the charity is deductible from the donor's gross taxable estate. In our firm, we explain that your gross taxable estate includes "everything you own, everything you control and everything your name is on." This means the value of your life insurance death benefit; retirement plan accounts, including IRAs, 401ks and 403bs; and all of your other assets. Also included is your interest in any property that may be jointly owned with another person (specifically including those assets owned as joint tenants with rights of survivorship). If there are income beneficiaries other than the donor and their spouse, there may be an estate tax on the value of this income interest.

The benefits of creating a charitable remainder annuity trust include the following:

- The donor can contribute a highly appreciated, low-income-producing asset to a charitable remainder annuity trust and receive a current income tax deduction. This could be especially beneficial to individuals who have accumulated large amounts of corporate stock at a low cost basis that pays only nominal dividend income.

※ The charitable remainder annuity trust can sell the highly appreciated asset without paying any capital gains tax and can then reinvest the entire proceeds at a higher rate of return.

※ The charitable remainder annuity trust will usually pay the designated income beneficiaries a higher rate of return than the donor previously received on the asset. This, coupled with the income tax deduction and the avoidance of the capital gains tax on the sale of the appreciated asset, can create a substantial increase in cash flow for the donor.

Charitable Remainder Unitrust

A charitable remainder unitrust (sometimes referred to as a CRUT) is an irrevocable trust which pays a fixed percentage of the value of its asset holdings each year to a named beneficiary such as the donor, their spouse, their children or others. For example, if $100,000 is donated to a six percent charitable remainder unitrust, the annual income stream the first year would be $6,000. In the second year, if the value of the trust assets grew to $110,000, the annual income stream would be $6,600. Likewise, if in the third year the value of the trust assets decline to $90,000, the annual income stream would be $5,400. Clearly, the income stream can fluctuate with the fluctuating value of the trust assets. After the death of the income beneficiaries or at the end of a predetermined number of years (no more than 20), the remaining trust assets are distributed by the trustee to the qualifying charity or charities named by the donor in the trust.

The trust assets are valued on an annual basis to determine the stream of income. Therefore, if the donor desires to add additional contributions in future years, this may be done and is easily accomplished. There is no necessity to create a new charitable remainder unitrust each time the donor wants to make an additional contribution.

The donor's charitable income tax deduction is determined utilizing the same analysis as for the charitable remainder annuity trust. Likewise, the gift tax and estate tax consequences and benefits are the same as for the charitable remainder annuity trust.

CHARITABLE LEAD TRUSTS

Property may be transferred to family members at low gift tax and estate tax rates by permitting income to be distributed to a charity over a period of years, and then later passed to family members. This type of irrevocable trust is called a charitable lead trust (sometimes referred to as a CLT). The charitable lead trust is the opposite of a charitable remainder trust because the trustee pays the income first to the charity and the remainder is distributed at the termination of the trust to family members or others. Properly drafted, charitable lead trusts can also result in a current income tax deduction to the donor.

Charitable lead trusts come in two popular varieties:
1) The charitable lead annuity trust (sometimes referred to as a CLAT) and;
2) The charitable lead unit trust (sometimes referred to as a CLUT).

The charitable lead annuity trust and charitable lead unitrust operate on the same income distribution principles as the charitable remainder annuity trust and charitable remainder unitrust. The primary difference between charitable remainder trusts and charitable lead trusts is the timing of the receipt of the charity's interest—today as an income stream or in the future as a remainder interest.

IRREVOCABLE LIFE INSURANCE TRUSTS (WEALTH REPLACEMENT TRUSTS)

Many tax advisors and financial planners recommend and use wealth replacement trusts (also referred to as irrevocable life insurance trusts, or ILITs) to replace assets or property given outright to charity or to a charitable remainder trust. A wealth replacement trust is created during the trustmaker[2]/donor's lifetime, utilizing life insurance purchased on the life of the trustmaker, or the trustmaker and their spouse, as the primary asset of the trust. The increased cash flow derived from charitable remainder trust planning (both the savings from the current income tax deduction as well as the increased income stream) can be used to fund the premium payments due on the life insurance. This technique can also be extremely valuable if the donor's retirement plan assets are used as the primary gift asset.

The use of this strategy allows a philanthropic donor to create a win-win situation. The charity wins and the donor's family also receives the benefit of a testamentary gift. Properly structured, the wealth replacement trust can provide an income tax-free and estate tax-free benefit to the donor's loved ones.

PRIVATE FOUNDATIONS

Although there are many benefits to charitable giving, one concern a donor may express is the loss of control over the money and/or property that is gifted to the charity. To overcome this concern, a donor can create an entity known as a private foundation that will distribute its donations and income to charitable causes favored by the donor or the donor's family.

A private foundation is a charitable organization created and funded by a donor (during life or at death) that is designed to achieve one or more specific charitable purposes. The overall management of the private foundation is provided by a board of directors or trustees often selected by the donor and frequently made up of the donor's family members. The directors or trustees can be paid reasonable compensation for their services.

An individual or a family may establish a private foundation to hold the family's charitable gifts. The donor can have complete discretion in distributing the funds to publicly supported qualifying organizations of their choice. Contributions to the private foundation qualify for income tax, estate tax and gift tax charitable deductions, subject to certain restrictions imposed by the Internal Revenue Service. Families who choose private foundations as part of their estate and family legacy plan retain maximum control over the distribution of their charitable gift assets and can use the private foundation to teach good stewardship to succeeding generations. A private foundation is another way to leave an enduring legacy for our family and our pets.

Federal tax law has specific legal and operating requirements to qualify a private foundation. Some of the most important requirements, which in turn make the proper administration of the private foundation critical, include:

- Failure to Distribute Income. If a private foundation fails to distribute its annual income by the end of the subsequent year, it is subject to a tax of 15 percent (Internal Revenue Code (IRC) Section 4942(a)). The tax can be increased to 100 percent if the income is not distributed by the date the tax is assessed or by the date the Internal Revenue Service issues a warning called a "90-day letter."

- Self Dealing. An excise tax can be triggered if a disqualified person—defined in the Internal Revenue Code as "an individual who is a substantial contributor to a foundation, a foundation manager, certain family members, related business entities, government officials, and others who hold a fiduciary capacity with regard to the foundation"—engages in restricted activities, including selling, exchanging or leasing property; lending money or providing credit; furnishing goods or services; paying compensation or reimbursing expenses; transferring foundation income or assets to or for the use of a disqualified person; or furnishing foundation money or property to a government official.

- Excess Business Holdings. A private foundation that possesses any excess business holdings is subject to a tax of five percent (IRC Section 4943(a)).

- Net Investment Income. A private foundation is liable for an excise tax of two percent on its net investment income (IRC Section 4940(a)).

- Investment Jeopardizes Charitable Purpose. An excise tax of five percent is imposed if the foundation invests its income and funds in such a way that its charitable purpose is jeopardized. (IRC Section 4944(a)).

- Legislative Activities. An excise tax of 10 percent is imposed if funds are used for legislative activities or for engaging in propaganda. In addition, foundation managers who authorize such expenditures can be liable for an additional two-and-a-half percent tax (IRC Section 4945(a)).

Clearly, a private foundation requires the guidance of many trusted advisors, including legal, financial, tax and charitable giving professionals. Not all families will have the temperament, the risk tolerance or the ability to effectively administer a family foundation. A family foundation, however, can be a valuable component of a family legacy plan that contemplates the elimination of the estate tax (called "zero tax estate planning").

SUPPORTING ORGANIZATIONS

An alternative to the private foundation is a supporting organization. The supporting organization has many of the advantages of a private foundation without many of the restrictions. The supporting organization is set up as a trust or nonprofit corporation. The donor retains influence over how charitable funds are used while enjoying the tax benefits allowed for donations to qualifying public charities.

A supporting organization, like a private foundation, is often established and funded by a single individual or family. Unlike private foundations, however, supporting organizations are afforded many of the benefits of being a public charity while avoiding the taxes and regulations imposed on private foundations.

A supporting organization which meets the requirements of IRC Section 509(a)(3) is distinguished from a private foundation as it serves public, rather than private, purposes. It is this public focus which justifies the organization's status as a "nonprivate" foundation.

A supporting organization is typically created as an irrevocable charitable trust. Occasionally, the donor will set up the organization as a nonprofit corporation under state law. At least one public charity (university, hospital, museum, humane society and so forth) must be identified in the organizing document as a recipient of the new organization's support. Frequently, the creator/donor and their family serve as trustees or directors of the supporting organization, along with the representatives of the charity or charities named.

There are three important tests to qualify as a supporting organization:

1) The supporting organization must operate exclusively for the benefit of one or more specified public charities.

2) The supporting organization must be operated, supervised or controlled by, or in connection with, one or more public charities.

3) The supporting organization must not be controlled (directly or indirectly) by a "disqualified person" as defined in IRC Section 4946 and discussed above in Private Foundations.

Generally, a supporting organization is accorded the benefits of being a public charity, including:

▒ Income Tax Deduction for Gifts. A supporting organization is treated the same from a tax perspective as for contributions to public charities.

▓ Not Subject to Private Foundation Excise Taxes. Specifically, the prohibitions against self-dealing, minimum distribution requirements, taxes on net investment income, excess business holdings, jeopardizing investments and prohibited expenditures that apply to private foundations do not apply to supporting organizations.

While many people focus on the tax benefits of charitable giving, others are primarily concerned with the loss of control over money and property gifted to a charity. For these persons, the private foundation is usually the preferred choice for achieving their philanthropic goals. The greater control found in a private foundation comes at a "cost" in the form of greater tax restrictions, significant administrative responsibilities and increased regulation.

While the creator of a supporting organization does not have the same level of control as the donor who establishes a private foundation, they can still have a significant voice in and impact on the organization.

An unspoken benefit of creating a supporting organization is the opportunity for a donor to involve their children and/or grandchildren in directing the family's philanthropic legacy to public charities in the community. By involving a younger generation in the organization, a donor is sometimes able to convey deeply held family values, while at the same time transferring funds to charitable causes.

DONOR ADVISED FUNDS

Donor advised funds, although not new in the charitable planning world, have recently grown in acceptance as a vehicle for the modern and moderate philanthropist.

A donor advised fund makes grants to public charities. The donor has the right to provide advice and recommendations with regard to grant recipients and also to the amount and timing of the grant. The donor is entitled to an immediate charitable contribution deduction upon making the contribution. The trustees of the fund are not obligated to follow the donor's advice and recommendations, although as a practical matter the donor generally expects they will.

Donor advised funds look very much like private foundations, though on a smaller scale. Like a private foundation, they conduct no charitable operations themselves, but instead fund other operating charities. They also provide the donor with an element of control similar to, but not identical to, that available through a private foundation.

POOLED INCOME FUND (PIF)

A pooled income fund (PIF) is similar to a charitable remainder trust except that more than one donor, as well as unrelated persons, are able to make contributions to the fund. A public charity establishes and maintains a common investment fund into which donors can transfer assets while retaining a share of the annual income in proportion to the donor's contributions.

The donor's federal income tax deduction is based on the ages of the beneficiaries and the highest rate of return paid by the fund over the last three years.[3] However, the frequency of payments does not affect the income tax deduction.

A pooled income fund may not invest in tax exempt securities nor accept them as contributions. Further, no donor or beneficiary may serve as a trustee. For those donors who desire to have an element of control through a role as trustee, a pooled income fund will not offer that opportunity.

If the donor causes the income to be paid to someone other than the donor, there is the potential for a taxable gift unless certain requirements are met and the income gift can qualify for the annual gift tax exclusion. The value of the asset passing to the pooled income fund is removed from the donor's gross estate for federal estate taxation purposes. The income stream received by the donor, however, could increase the donor's estate unless otherwise spent, gifted or consumed. As with a charitable remainder trust, after the life income beneficiaries die, the remaining assets pass to the pooled income fund charity.

CHARITABLE GIFT ANNUITY (CGA)

A charitable gift annuity makes it possible to transfer cash or marketable securities, such as stocks or bonds (including mutual funds), to a charity in exchange for fixed payments (like an annuity) that the donor or someone else the donor designates will receive for life.

The amount of the annual income received is determined based on the age of the income beneficiary. The older the donor, the higher the income received. For older individuals on a fixed income, the charitable gift annuity may be the best way to increase lifetime income while providing a testamentary benefit to a loved charity.

From an income tax perspective, the donor gets a current income tax deduction based on the future value of the gift to the charity. In addition, the income stream received may also receive favorable income tax treatment depending on its characterization as interest, capital gains or return of principal.

CHARITABLE REMAINDER PET TRUSTS

Discussed above are the traditional charitable planning techniques. However, on May 10, 2001, Rep. Earl Blumenauer (D-Ore.) introduced H.R. 1796, also known as the Morgan Bill (named after the drafting attorney's pet collie) that, if enacted, would amend section 664 of the Internal Revenue Code to permit the creation of a "charitable remainder pet trust." This charitable remainder pet trust would operate in a manner similar to conventional charitable remainder trusts, with income payable for the exclusive benefit of one or more pets for a term of not more than 20 years or for the life or lives of such pet or pets. Ultimately, the remainder interest would be paid to a qualifying charitable organization under section 170(C). The bill would also modify Internal Revenue Code (IRC) Sections 170, 2522 and 2055 to recognize this new type of trust for income tax, gift tax and estate tax deduction purposes.

The Morgan Bill also includes a provision that the term "pet" for purposes of a charitable remainder pet trust is "any domesticated companion animal (including a domesticated companion cat, dog, rabbit, guinea pig, hamster, gerbil, ferret, mouse, rat, bird, fish, reptile, or horse) which is living, and owned or cared for by the taxpayer establishing the trust, at the time of the creation of the trust."

One tongue in cheek expression of concern is how you would calculate the present value of a remainder interest for a cat. Would you use one life or nine? In addition, it appears, any taxes on distributions from the pet trust would be paid by the charitable remainder trust, thereby relieving the pet of the responsibility of completing its own income tax return. (Thank goodness. My cats are terrible at math!)

It appears this proposed change would apply only to charitable remainder annuity trusts (CRATs) and charitable remainder unitrusts (CRUTs) and not to pooled income funds or charitable gift annuities.

Under current law[1], a charitable remainder trust that names a pet as an income recipient or pays income for the benefit of a pet may, depending on local law, have the following results:

- Be deemed valid and enforceable,
- Be valid but unenforceable, or
- Be void from the inception.

In all cases, however, the transfer to the pet would not be deductible for income tax, gift tax or estate tax deduction purposes. Therefore, no qualified charitable remainder trust would exist. At present, the Morgan Bill remains pending before the House Ways and Means Committee, and no further action has been taken.

ESTATE AND GIFT TAX REVENUE RECONCILIATION ACT (EGTRRA)

In June 2001, the Estate and Gift Tax Revenue Reconciliation Act (EGTRRA) was passed, making significant changes to the income tax, estate tax and gift tax rules. What effect these new rules will have on a donor's future willingness to make charitable gifts will remain to be seen. It seems clear, however, that in light of September 11, 2001, additional significant tax law changes will occur in the future that could make the June 2001 changes obsolete.

Keep in mind that even if estate taxes and gift taxes were wholly eliminated (not likely to happen, if at all, or for long), there are numerous non-tax reasons to do proper estate planning, family legacy planning and charitable gift giving. In our practice, we always try to "keep the tax tail from wagging the estate planning dog." Some non-tax reasons to do proper estate tax planning include:

- Guardianship avoidance.
- Probate avoidance.
- Bequests to special-needs children.
- Bequests to pets.
- Personal planning protections, such as remarriage protection, divorce protection, catastrophic illness protection, catastrophic accident protection, protection from creditors, incentive planning or value transfer planning for loved ones, to name just a few.
- Control estate administration and settlement costs.
- Asset investment and administration.

TRUST ADMINISTRATION

In all instances of charitable planning, the administration of the trust assets is critical to the success of the trust. For privately created charitable trusts, trust administration should be performed by a licensed professional (like a certified public accountant) or a professional trust administration company. Proper trust administration can provide the following benefits:

- Strict attention to all compliance and tax-reporting issues.
- Custody and sale of gifted assets.
- Cost basis recorded for gifted assets.
- Calculation of income tax charitable deduction.
- Calculation of estate tax charitable deduction.
- Calculation of annual trust values to determine income beneficiary distributions.
- Revaluation of trust based on added contributions.

- Inventory of all trust assets, their fair market value and cost basis.

- A record of all trust transactions based on a four-tier accounting system.

- A record of all dividend, interest and principal payments.

- Daily cash sweeps to taxable or tax-free money market investments.

- Coordination and payment of distributions to all income beneficiaries.

- Preparation of final accounting at the termination or end of the trust.

- Distribution of remaining assets to the qualifying charity or charities.

There is an unlimited number of ways charitable giving can be incorporated into your estate plan or family legacy plan. The best choice for you and your family will depend on a number of factors, not the least of which is your commitment to philanthropy. Always work with your professional advisors to determine the estate planning, legacy planning and charitable planning strategies that will work best for you.

---

1 This would not necessarily be true if the donor's spouse was not a United States citizen.

2 The term "trustmaker" is used rather than the legal jargon of "settlor," "grantor" or "trustor."

3 See Rev. Rul. 94-41, I. R. B. 1994-26.5.

4 See Rev. Rul. 78-105.

Animal Care Organizations

There are a number of animal care organizations in existence today dedicated to the short-term, long-term or perpetual care of pets that can no longer be cared for by their owners. Some of these organizations are referred to as shelters, perpetual care facilities or long-term care animal sanctuaries.

If an organization rather than an individual caregiver is your best long-term care alternative, the selection of the organization will be critical to the health, happiness and well-being of your pet. This chapter is designed to provide you with some of the options that are available as well as a checklist of information you will want to obtain as you evaluate your possible alternatives.

Some organizations will accept and provide continuing care for your pet; others will permanently place your pet in a home or in a "foster care" program until a permanent home can be found. Some long-term care facilities are not-for-profit organizations that qualify as charitable organizations under the requirements for a 501(c)(3) organization, and your donations may be tax deductible. Others are not recognized charities, and any donations to these organizations will not provide the donor with any income tax or estate tax advantages.

Application fees, kennel fees, placement fees, medical care costs, disposition after the death of your pet and other expenses will vary from organization to organization. Health certificates may be required prior to acceptance. This requirement may put pets and owners at a disadvantage if the pet cannot be certified healthy at the time of placement. Depending on your choice of facility, if your pet must be transported across state lines, additional health certifications or medical care may have to be obtained or provided before your pet can be transported. Some programs may require the spaying or neutering of your pet at or prior to acceptance, yet some may agree to continue existing breeding programs within specific limitations.

Many facilities are designed to care for "usual" domesticated pets like cats, dogs, hamsters, guinea pigs, rabbits and horses. But what happens if your pet is a reptile, a spider or a type not typically provided for at this facility? Carefully consider your choices if your pet is not of the "usual" variety.

Some organizations have calculated their costs based on the average life expectancy of your pet. I have seen projected costs for a cat quoted at $1,100 per year for normal care. A note of caution here: It is important to ascertain in writing how the organization defines "normal" care so that you can evaluate whether this is consistent with your definition of the type of care you want your pet to receive. I found one organization that accepts donations based on a table that varies with the age of the donor, not the pet.

If your funds run out and are not sufficient for the continued care of your pet, what will happen to your pet at that time? Some organizations will agree to accept your pet even if you do not have sufficient funds to donate for your pet's long-term care. However, others require sufficient funds in advance. If the funds run out, your pet may be out of luck. If you have a "special needs" pet that requires additional care because the animal is blind, deaf, paralyzed or missing limbs or eyes, or because your requirements for care exceed what the facility considers to be normal or usual, you can expect additional charges that could run into hundreds of dollars per month and thousands of dollars annually. One organization quotes an "extra special care" fee of $250 per month, or $2,750 per year. Fortunately, some organizations will accept your donation or care fees utilizing a major credit card. Each facility is vastly different, and I know of no organization providing oversight or certification of long-term care facilities for domestic animals.

The choice of a long-term or perpetual care facility for your pet should not be made without proper due diligence and investigation. Some of these facilities or sanctuaries advertise themselves as "no-kill" facilities that will care for your pet even if it is considered "unadoptable." Others may place your pet in a suitable permanent or foster care home until a permanent home can be located. Still others make their animals available to anyone willing to adopt a pet, often without any follow-up program or procedures. Some of these facilities have been targeted by medical research organizations involved in various cruelty industries as an easy, low-cost source of research animals. I can think of few things sadder than a family pet becoming part of any kind of research project.

Don't overlook a nearby veterinary college as a potential source of long-term care for your pet. I discovered one program sponsored by Kansas State University's College of Veterinary Medicine. The program is called Perpetual Pet Care and allows pet owners to set up an endowed scholarship for a veterinary student who will, in turn, care for the pet in case the owner becomes incapacitated or predeceases their pet. In order to qualify for the program, a veterinary student has to be in good academic standing and express an interest in the type of pet specified. If the student meets the established criteria, they will be eligible to receive a scholarship created by the program.

The pet owner may specify the type of housing and food the pet will have, the amount of exercise and playtime the pet enjoys, and the extent and nature of the medical care they want the student to provide for the pet. Pets in the program would undoubtedly have access to medical care provided by the Kansas State Veterinary Medical Teaching Hospital.

The owner can also determine if they want their pet to remain with one owner or whether their pet should be transferred to another student after the graduation of the scholarship recipient. Remaining funds after the completion of the program, presumably at the end of the pet's natural life, would be used for the College of Veterinary Medicine and the Pet Trust. The Pet Trust is described as a fund that supports studies on diseases and disorders in animals. The Pet Trust's stated purpose is also to help improve the quality of veterinary medical education at Kansas State.

ANIMAL CARE ORGANIZATION CHECKLIST

Before you decide on a long-term care facility for your pet, be sure to evaluate the organization carefully. I have prepared a checklist that may be helpful in organizing your thoughts for selecting one of these facilities as a long-term care solution for your pet:

1) Visit the shelter or facility.

2) What are the living conditions (cages, open-area rooms, runs, pastures, paddocks, stalls, etc.)?

   a. How many animals are maintained in each situation?

   b. How much playtime or interaction do the animals have with humans?

   c. How much playtime or interaction do they have with other animals?

   d. What are the animals' exercise opportunities? Are these consistent with your pet's requirements? With your requirements?

     e. What types of food are the animals fed? How often? Can you influence the food choices?

        i. Does your pet have special dietary need considerations?

        ii. How are treats regulated?

3) What types of pets does the facility accept?

     a. Will they accept the type of pet you have?

     b. Will they accept your pet regardless of its age or medical needs?

4) What type of veterinary care is provided?

     a. Are you familiar with the veterinarian or veterinary clinic providing services?

     b. How long has the veterinarian or the veterinary clinic been affiliated with the organization?

     c. Are examinations scheduled on a regular basis (semi-annual, annual, as needed)?

     d. Is dental care provided? How often?

     e. What other types of routine care are provided?

     f. How are the costs of veterinary care handled? Are they included as part of your donation/payment?

     g. How are the extraordinary care requirements handled?

5) What kind of staff does the facility employ?

     a. How many?

     b. Full-time?

     c. Part-time?

     d. Volunteers?

     e. Is there any kind of training program for the staff or volunteers?

    f. Do any employees have special skills or training?

6) How long has the facility been in business?

    a. What are its sources of funding?

    b. Is it a "for-profit" or "not-for-profit" organization?

    c. Are your payments/donations tax deductible?

7) How much will the long-term care of your pet cost?

    a. Does the facility require a lump-sum payment?

    b. Are payments made during the lifetime of your pet?

    c. How are these costs calculated?

    d. Are they guaranteed?

    e. What happens to your pet if your donation/payment is insufficient to cover costs?

8) What is the facility's succession plan in the event it must go out of business?

    a. Who will take care of your pet?

    b. What will happen to the money you have donated?

9) Have their been any complaints to the Better Business Bureau or local chamber of commerce?

10) Will the facility provide references? If so, diligently investigate these references. If not, consider another choice.

11) Will your pet be available for adoption or foster care, or is the care designed for your pet's life?

    a. In the event your pet is adopted, what type of follow-up program does the facility have?

    b. If the adoptive family can no longer keep your pet, what is the facility's policy in regard to returning the animal?

12) How will your pet be provided for in the event it becomes ill?
    a. What is the facility's policy on long-term care?
    b. What is the facility's position on euthanasia?
    c. How many persons are involved in a euthanasia decision?
    d. What type of euthanasia procedure do they use?
    e. Will they honor your request for an animal care panel?
13) How will your pet be provided for after its death?
    a. Burial
    b. Cremation
    c. Further disposition
    d. Can you direct the disposition of your pet after its death?

There may be instances when the placement and on-going or perpetual care of your pet may not be consistent with your wishes. In some cases, the kindest wish we can have for our pet in the event of our disability or death is humane euthanasia. There are some animals that, as a result of age, health or temperament, would not be easily or successfully placed in an alternate care environment. In some cases, forcing a pet to adjust to a new person or new circumstances can compound the pet's suffering. However, this is a choice that only a loving owner can make, keeping the best interests of the pet in mind. Consultation with your veterinarian and family members is highly recommended.

CONTRACT CONSIDERATIONS

Entering into a perpetual care contract for your pet is the same as entering into any other kind of contract. You need to do your homework in advance, and you should always have a qualified attorney review the contract before signing. Make sure the contract clearly identifies the parties and the costs, clearly identifies and recites your expectations with regard to the care requirements for your pet, clearly identifies and recites your expectations for the placement of your pet (if desired or permitted), and clearly states what will happen to your pet in the event the facility closes, you run out of money, or your pet dies. All of the terms and conditions should be included in the contract. Do not rely on the representations of any employee or owner of a facility—get it in writing!

SELECTING A CHARITY

In a recent article, by Jon Newberry (*ABA Journal*/July 2001) entitled "Checking Up on Charities," the author commented that individuals were responsible for more than 75 percent of the $190 billion dollars in charitable contributions in 1999. For many donors, a critical issue regarding whether they will donate at all will be an ability to determine whether the money they have donated will be used in the way they intend. The BBB Wise Giving Alliance reports there are more than 740,0000 charities recognized by the Internal Revenue Service, with an additional 30,000 new charities recognized each year.

I have provided a checklist to provide guidance in evaluating charities to which you may be contemplating contributions.

CHARITY EVALUATION CHECKLIST

Is the charity what it claims to be?

Many organizations have names that sound alike. You might believe the American Humane Society is the same as The Humane Society of the United States. Make sure the organization you are dealing with is actually the organization you think it is. Do your homework in advance. Be wary of organizations you are unfamiliar with that solicit contributions over the telephone and then are unwilling to provide any information regarding the charity prior to getting your commitment for a donation. Legitimate charitable organizations are happy to provide a copy of their latest annual report at any time.

The annual report prepared by the charity will generally provide a mission statement, detail the organization's finances (including receipts and expenditures) for the most recent year, provide the names of the persons serving on the board of directors, and describe the organization's current programs and results.

Is my contribution tax deductible?

To qualify as a tax-exempt organization under the Internal Revenue Service rules for 501(c)(3) organizations, a charitable organization, with annual gross receipts in excess of $5,000, must apply for and obtain recognition of tax-exempt status from the Internal Revenue Service. There are exceptions to this general rule. An organization qualifies as a tax-exempt charitable organization if it is organized and operated exclusively for charitable purposes, serves public rather than private interests, and refrains from engaging in any political activity or significant amounts of lobbying activity.

To make sure your contribution is tax deductible, ask the organization for confirmation of its status as a tax-exempt organization. Donations to organizations that do not qualify for an exemption under 501(c)(3) may be disallowed on your income tax return. In addition, contributions to foreign organizations are generally not tax-deductible on your income tax return, unless permitted by a tax treaty.

Will the charity spend my money wisely?

There are a number of ways to check on the administration and operating efficiency of the tax-exempt charitable organization you are considering. You can do the research yourself and review the organization's IRS Form 990, you can ask the organization directly, or you can rely on watchdog groups that analyze the performance of many large national charities. Of course, if the charity you are considering is not large enough to attract the attention of an oversight organization, you will have to do your own analysis of the documentation you are able to discover during your research.

Watchdog groups point out that fundraising efficiency is not always the best measure of an organization's worthiness or commitment to the cause they serve. Newer charities and charities that support less-publicized causes often have a harder time raising funds than the larger, well-established charities do, yet they may actually be providing valuable charitable services. Charities that operate on a smaller scale may actually utilize more of your donation dollars for the cause you want to support, rather than toward fundraising and administrative efforts. It is important to note that fundraising is a primary goal of most nonprofit organizations, and it would be unwise to hold fundraising efforts against them. However, analyzing the effectiveness of a charity's fundraising efforts would certainly be prudent. Do your homework and you be the judge.

Where do I start?

The beginning point of any financial analysis of a charity is often IRS Form 990, an annual statement required to be filed with the IRS. The report details sources of funds received, use of funds expended and changes in assets and liabilities.

Anyone may obtain a copy of an organization's exemption application or annual information return, Form 990. A request can be made directly to the organization or by submitting a request to the Internal Revenue Service on Form

4506-A. You may also be able to access a charity's IRS Form 990 on the Internet.

For more information about what to look for when evaluating a charity, you can request Internal Revenue Service Publication 1771, Charitable Contributions (for exempt organizations)—Substantiation and Disclosure Requirements. This form can be downloaded at the Internal Revenue Service web site or by calling the IRS at (800) 829-3676.

Religious organizations and groups that take in less than $25,000 a year are exempt from filing Form 990, but most other nonprofit organizations have to file Form 990 each year. Copies of the filings are available on a number of web sites, including the National Center for Charitable Statistics at www.nccs.urban.org. As a side note, even private charitable organizations such as a family foundation may be required to file Form 990 annually.

RESOURCES TO EVALUATE CHARITIES

There are a number of organizations dedicated to evaluating and maintaining statistics on charitable organizations. I have listed a few of them here:

- The Internal Revenue Service maintains a web site at www.irs.ustreas.gov. Look at the link for "Exempt Organizations" on the "Tax Info for You" page.
- Philanthropic Research Inc. Find them on the Internet at www.Guidestar.org. They provide information on more than 700,000 nonprofit organizations.

- American Institute of Philanthropy (AIP). The American Institute of Philanthropy rates nonprofit groups based on the percentage of total expenses that go to programs (as opposed to fundraising efforts or administration) and on their fundraising efficiency. Find them on the Internet at www.charitywatch.org.
- National Charities Information Bureau (NCIB).
- The Better Business Bureau (BBB) publishes detailed reports on hundreds of national charities. These reports can be obtained for free by mail or through its web site at www.bbb.org.

Choosing an Estate Planning Attorney

S electing the right estate planning attorney for you means doing your homework—educating yourself, defining your needs, learning to value professional services and seeking guidance in the selection of a qualified individual. Proper estate planning and legacy planning revolves around your relationship with your attorney.

Unfortunately, there are many businesses and salespeople masquerading as estate planning professionals. They are inundating the public with sales schemes that involve selling wills, living trusts and other estate planning documents without the involvement of attorneys in the counselling, design and drafting of the documents. They are the opposite of what my partner and I, along with our colleagues in the National Network of Estate Planning Attorneys, represent. Our approach is consistent with the implementation of a Three Step Strategy™—working with a counselling-oriented attorney, establishing and maintaining a formal updating program, and assuring fully disclosed and controlled settlement costs. For us, this is the recipe for an estate plan that works!

Proper estate planning requires professional thoroughness by attorneys and other advisors and respect for the overall well-being of the client and the client's family, including their pets. We aspire to the highest ethical professional behavior that will lend dignity to the client, the planning professional and the planning process.

In evaluating your needs and finding a qualified attorney, consider the following:

WHAT IS AN ATTORNEY?

Attorneys are known by many different names, such as lawyer, counselor or counsellor, solicitor and advocate. Attorneys are required to obtain extensive educational training in order to be prepared and able to represent a client. To qualify to practice law, attorneys must earn a law degree—referred to as a Juris Doctor or J.D.—pass a state bar examination and commit to pursuing continuing legal education for the duration of their legal career.

Attorneys are subject to codes of ethical conduct and professional responsibility imposed by their state bar associations. Generally, the profession as a whole self-monitors its members. Attorneys can be sole practitioners, members of small firms or members of large firms. An attorney can be an associate or a partner. Attorneys can be general practitioners (sometimes referred to by other attorneys as "threshold attorneys"—they take anyone as a client who can cross the threshold!) or attorneys can specialize in a particular area of the law. Beware: My partner and I have never met an attorney who didn't feel qualified to draft a will. Experience has taught us the result could be similar to asking your eye doctor to do open heart surgery!

Attorneys can be plaintiff oriented or defense oriented. They can be trial attorneys, called litigators, where they have a practice that focuses on trial work, or they can be transactional lawyers who concentrate on some of the non-litigation aspects of the law, such as corporate, real estate or estate planning. Then there are attorneys who refer to themselves, as my partner and I do, as "relationship" attorneys. In our estate planning practice, we are not interested in a client for a single transactional event but, instead, for the client's lifetime, in an ongoing, mutually rewarding and beneficial relationship.

Selecting an attorney will depend on many different factors—not the least of which is the purpose for which you are interviewing attorneys in the first place. It is important to think about attorneys in the same context as doctors. You would not hire your family practitioner or gynecologist to conduct brain surgery despite the fact they both went to medical school and have the same underlying educational foundation. The same is true for attorneys. Additional training and years of specialization are determining factors in selecting the right professional for your legal needs.

Selecting the right attorney is critical. However, just seeking a competent attorney is often not enough. Consider the personal qualities your attorney should have before you start interviewing candidates. Things you should look for:

- Scrupulous honesty and integrity.
- Sensitive and perceptive communication.
- Good judgment and common sense.
- Discipline and toughness.
- Creativity in finding constructive solutions.
- Bar affiliations, designations, advanced training, specialization and professional associations.
- Attitude toward creating a legacy for your pet.

WHAT DOES "BOARD CERTIFIED" MEAN?

Board certification is a voluntary designation program for attorneys. Certification requirements vary depending on your state and the specialty in which the attorney is seeking certification. Certification often requires additional continuing legal education requirements and may require the applicant to pass an additional certification examination. There may be additional requirements that the attorney has practiced in the specialty area for a number of years; devotes a required percentage of practice to the specialty area; handles a variety of matters in the specialty area to demonstrate experience and involvement; attends continuing education in the specialty area; obtains evaluations by fellow lawyers and judges; and passes a written examination.

Some attorneys seek out board certification as recognition of their expertise in a particular specialty area. Other attorneys feel their skill and expertise is sufficient without further certification. In some instances, professional liability premiums may increase, as the board-certified attorney may be held to a higher standard of competence.

WHY DO I EVEN NEED AN ATTORNEY — CAN'T I DO MY OWN ESTATE PLAN?

You can try. Many have. Everyone already has an estate plan, whether they know it or not. Generally, for married couples, it consists of joint ownership with rights of survivorship. For single individuals, it may also consist of joint ownership, but with another individual, either a friend or perhaps a child. Beyond joint ownership, most people utilize beneficiary designations for life insurance and retirement plans for the transfer of their assets at death.

However, if you ask, "Does a 'do-it-myself' plan work for my family?" and you answer, "No," then you have made progress in recognizing that the laws of the United States are complex and you should seriously consider the guidance and advice of a professional. It pays to select your estate planning professional with care since you will not survive to see whether your plan succeeds and your loved ones will live with the results!

Your legal professional has spent thousands of dollars and years of time learning how to analyze problems and how to distinguish the simple from the complex. Finding a simple solution to a complex problem has as much value as unraveling a complex situation that may appear simple. Professionals add value to their services by their knowledge, skill and wisdom, continuing education, independent perspective and willingness to take responsibility for the results.

OKAY, I AM CONVINCED I NEED AN ATTORNEY. HOW DO I FIND THE ONE WHO WILL BE BEST FOR ME?

This is a serious, but not necessarily difficult, task. First, consider recommendations from friends and other attorneys. Personal referrals are generally the best way to find out about any type of service you might need, and legal representation is no exception. Talk to other people who are similarly situated. Ask your banker, your veterinarian, your local animal shelter, your financial advisor or your current legal services provider. Attorneys rely on good client relations and word-of-mouth reference for generating business. If you don't have any success getting a personal referral, consider the local or state bar associations or other legal referral services. Consider contacting professional organizations like the National Network of Estate Planning Attorneys for an individual qualified in your state.

The *Martindale Hubbell Law Directory* is also a recognized source of information about attorneys. There are many other directories which list attorneys; however, remember that often the attorneys listed in the directory have paid a fee for the privilege of being listed there. As a last resort, "let your fingers do the walking" and search your local yellow pages.

WHAT KIND OF QUESTIONS SHOULD I ASK?

You should ask questions pertinent to your particular area of concern, and you should focus on the following:

* What is your experience in this field?
* Have you handled matters like mine?
* What are the possible problems or concerns in situations like mine?
* How long do you expect this matter to take?
* How will you communicate with me?
* Will you be my only contact or will someone else be working with you?
* Is there a charge for the initial consultation?
* How do you handle your legal fees? Do you charge by the project? Do you charge a percentage? Do you charge by the hour? What is your hourly rate? How many hours do you expect this will take?
* Beyond fees, what types of expenses do you expect to incur?
* If I need to make changes, how will the fees be handled?
* When will I be asked to pay? How often will I receive a bill? If fees are not paid on time, will interest accrue?

- What alternative recommendations can you make?
- Will I sign a formal fee or engagement agreement?
- In the event of a dispute, do you recommend mediation, arbitration or litigation?
- How will you keep my plan updated and current?
- How much will you charge my estate in the event of my disability or death?

With regard to legal fees and costs, it is important to understand the fees and billing arrangement before you get a bill. Attorneys' fees can vary dramatically depending on the nature and scope of the legal services provided. The scope of the representation is an understanding as to what the attorney will do (or not do), how long it will take, what the attorney will not do without further authorization, what the client's goals are and so forth. Financial arrangements should be as clear as possible, unless doing so would take longer than whatever it is the attorney is being retained to do. Even then, the maxim is "Put it in writing."

There are a number of factors that may enter into the calculation of an attorney's fees. Some attorneys provide services on a percentage basis, contingency, flat-fee or quoted-fee basis while others provide services based on an hourly calculation which becomes a function of the attorney's (and their staff's) hourly billing rate multiplied by the number of hours expended on your behalf. If you have legal needs of an ongoing nature, will the attorney agree to a retainer-fee agreement in which you pay a fixed fee each month for services? Are costs included in the quoted fee or will they be in addition to any quoted amounts? Are there any other add-on fees or costs, like legal research fees, paralegal costs, long distance phone charges or facsimile and copy charges?

Higher hourly fees generally coincide with an attorney's experience and/or their geographic location. For example, an attorney in Los Angeles, Chicago, New York City or Washington, D.C. is likely to charge a higher hourly rate than a comparable attorney in a smaller city. Likewise, the size of the firm may dictate higher hourly rates for both partners and associates than would a smaller firm in the same location. Other factors that play into higher fees are the cost of rent, salaries for support staff, and firm "perks" or benefits.

Generally, fees are negotiable although, as a rule, not after the services have been provided. If you intend to negotiate with your attorney for the value of the services provided, it would be best to initiate that conversation prior to the onset of the representation. Alternatively, some attorneys may be offended by the notion they would consider negotiating their fees and may be unwilling to compromise on their fees.

As with any other situation in which you will be contracting for professional services, I recommend you obtain, review and execute a fee agreement or engagement letter which clearly outlines the scope of the representation provided and the billing arrangement to which you have agreed. Make sure you understand your rights with regard to termination of the relationship and what will happen in the event of a dispute between you and your attorney. Further, make sure you understand how long the attorney intends to maintain your file. Does the attorney have any processes or procedures for keeping you updated in the event the law changes with regard to the services previously provided? My experience is that most encounters with an attorney are on a transactional basis. This means the legal relationship for representation purposes is terminated when the scope of the transaction is completed. Others, however, are interested in and are firmly committed to developing long-term, mutually beneficial relationships.

HOW DO I MAKE SURE MY ATTORNEY AND I HAVE A GOOD RELATIONSHIP?

Good legal assistance and advice is not a one-way street. You have to cooperate with your attorney if you genuinely want them to help you. The attorney-client relationship is privileged and confidential, so you need to take a lawyer into your confidence. Here are some important tips:

Don't withhold information from your attorney. In the field of estate planning, it is critical your attorney know everything about you and your loved ones, including all of your hopes, dreams, fears, aspirations, eccentricities and peccadilloes. Your attorney needs to know what it is like to be you or a member of your family. What does life look like for your loved ones if you are disabled or if you pass away?

What assets do you own, how do you own them and who are the named beneficiaries? What type of planning have you done in the past? Without all of the information, the attorney will be unable to assess your situation, educate you about the law and how it affects you and your family, and achieve a result that will be in your best interest.

Don't expect simple or immediate answers to complicated questions or circumstances. Attorneys are justifiably cautious in drawing conclusions or answering complex legal questions without consideration of all the relevant facts. An attorney knows there can be a number of alternative answers to the same question and the law is rarely an "open and shut" case. Attorneys have also been trained to closely examine both sides of an argument. You may find that attorneys frequently use "lawyer words" like "it depends," "possibly," "could be," "there is a great likelihood." Rarely will attorneys use statements such as "always" and "never." There are frequently a large number of factors that can cause any situation to have an unintended or unexpected outcome.

Keep your attorney advised of all new developments. In order to do a good job, your attorney needs to be apprised of facts that may have changed in your personal or financial situation. When your attorney has all the facts, they can use this information to provide you with relevant information regarding changes in the law or the attorney's experience.

Never hesitate to ask your attorney about anything you believe is relevant to your situation. Your attorney cannot read your mind. Also, remember that attorneys are not psychiatrists, doctors, marriage counselors, certified public accountants or financial advisors, unless they have specialized training. You may still need a team of trusted advisors to provide you with answers to all of your relevant questions and concerns.

Follow your attorney's advice. You asked for it, you paid good money for it. Don't work against your attorney.

Be patient. Don't expect instant results. Trust your attorney to follow through and follow up, but don't hesitate to ask for periodic progress reports. You have a right to know exactly what your attorney is doing for you. If you have engaged the services of an estate planning attorney who practices utilizing a systematic estate planning process, you should always know what to expect next.

Your attorney's primary obligation is to you. Their interest is protecting your rights and providing you with the highest possible quality of service. Early consultation with an attorney can save you trouble, time and money because:

- The solution to your legal situation may be easily resolved or prevented entirely, depending on the nature of your problem.

- The earlier you seek competent advice, the less time generally needed to complete the work required.
- Information is generally more readily available when prompt action is taken. Within the estate planning realm, this may be especially important in the event a person becomes mentally disabled or catastrophically ill or dies before they have completed their planning.
- Many legal matters or strategies are time sensitive or may have a "statute of limitations." Failure to act in a timely manner may prevent you from acting at all.

WHAT OTHER THINGS SHOULD I CONSIDER?

Experience. The length of time an attorney has been in practice is an important indicator of their success and ability to adequately handle your legal matter. Most attorneys require between three and five years of experience before they have gained reasonable competence in a particular area of the law.

Background. Does the attorney have any specific background or experiences that provide them with a unique perspective on your situation? Many attorneys are "second career" individuals who may have worked in other professional areas prior to attending law school. This past professional experience may lend significant insight and expertise to their area of practice.

Comfort. How does the attorney make you feel? Do you feel comfortable and understood? Does the attorney speak in language you can understand? Do they take the time to explain those questions that are still unclear to you? Is the attorney willing to include your pets as part of your estate plan?

Work load. What is the attorney's work load? Ask the attorney how many clients they are currently handling. Are they feeling overwhelmed by their work load or outside commitments? What other projects are they working on? What are their outside interests? Do you feel rushed? Is the attorney taking the time to fully answer all questions regarding your situation? Has the attorney explained the retainer or fee agreement? Do you feel pressured to sign the retainer and run out of the office?

Past results. Past results are never a guarantee of future success, but knowing an attorney's track record or experience in your type of situation can provide added comfort if they have had continuing success in cases similar in nature to yours. Ask whether the attorney is committed to creating an estate plan that works.

Professional liability insurance. Some state laws and some state bar ethics rules require that an attorney include information in their retainer agreements regarding their professional liability coverage. Professional liability insurance is designed to protect you from negligence or intentional behavior of your attorney that produces an undesirable result.

Some attorneys may include information concerning their professional liability coverage in your written retainer agreement. If not, you can ask whether they are sufficiently protected. If an attorney does not carry professional liability insurance, you may pay lower fees. However, if a material mistake is made on your case which affects the intended or desired outcome, you may have legal recourse but no ability to recover financial damages from the attorney's personal resources.

Imagination. Look for the attorney's ability to imagine ways in which something might go wrong. In our practice, my partner and I have a philosophy of "planning for the worst and hoping for the best" because any other kind of plan is simply wishful thinking. If something can go wrong it will, and Murphy's Law generally ensures that the one thing that was not planned for is the one thing that will happen.

Skill. Skill includes familiarity with the law, with a technical field or with legal procedures. Skill cannot be taken for granted. Although attorneys have different skills and skill levels, *any* attorney is legally permitted to handle any legal matter, so long as: 1) there is no conflict of interest; 2) the attorney can handle the matter competently (generally a matter of opinion—the attorney's); and 3) all other laws and rules of professional conduct are followed.

Like other skilled professionals, attorneys develop skills in specific areas of practice. An attorney who is very skilled at matters of type X may need to climb a steep learning curve to properly handle a matter of type Y. Beware of general practitioners or those who have a threshold practice because these individuals, although they may be very good at some legal matters, may not have the specific expertise you need or require. As mentioned, my partner and I have discovered that many attorneys, regardless of their practice area, feel competent to draft a "simple" will. Our experience has been, and continues to be, that there is no such thing as a "simple" estate plan, only clients and professionals who don't fully understand the enormity of the problem.

Noted professional coach Dan Sullivan has said, "The number one way to expand opportunity is by educating the client. Get them off their fixation that they know what the solution is to their problem. The reason they have the problem is they don't understand. The reason they don't have the solution is they don't know what the problem is. Educate them on the real problem—the solution is larger than they realize. Therein lies the opportunity."

Problems are often greater than we realize because of a lack of educated wisdom. A professional has an obligation to utilize their education, experience and wisdom to properly educate clients about all their options and opportunities. Only then can you, the client, participate in a meaningful encounter that will result in a comprehensive estate and legacy plan for your family.

Intuition, or "good instincts." Intuition may arise from previous encounters with a judge, an opposing attorney, a unique understanding of human nature or information regarding some other decision maker in the matter at hand. Intuition can give an attorney a sense of how a decision maker is likely to react to various arguments being considered or what strategy or technique is required to accomplish the desired result. There may be no way to determine whether someone has good intuition, except to rely on your *own* intuition.

Good character. This concept is complementary to intuition, but, of course, good character and reputation are necessary components to a successful attorney-client relationship. Attorneys rely on their good character and reputation for increased and repeat relationships with clients.

Other factors that will also be important include the resources available to the attorney, the amount of time the attorney can spend on your matter and so on. Ultimately, you must be comfortable with your attorney because your attorney cannot help you unless you can effectively communicate with each other. Choose someone you respect, not someone who intimidates you or uses jargon when it is not needed or required. Your calls should be answered promptly and professionally. Your concerns should be handled with empathy and respect. You should not feel as if conversations with your attorney are being either rushed or dragged out. If you are not comfortable, let your attorney know. If the relationship doesn't improve, look elsewhere.

WHAT IF I CAN'T AFFORD A LAWYER?

Don't assume you can't afford a lawyer. Investigate the matter with competent legal counsel first. In many instances, the cost of competent legal advice now can save you hundreds, if not thousands, of dollars later. If you still feel you cannot afford legal help, you may want to consult your local legal aid society for assistance. Many attorneys are required as part of their bar membership to provide free or *pro bono* service to local legal aid societies. Don't assume that because you are utilizing the services of a legal aid society you will not receive quality legal assistance.

NATIONAL NETWORK OF ESTATE PLANNING ATTORNEYS (NNEPA)

The National Network of Estate Planning Attorneys is a cooperative alliance of approximately 1,000 nationally recognized estate planning attorneys from across the country. Together, they provide one another with the support, education and tools they need to serve their clients better while building highly successful and rewarding practices.

Founded by leading educators and estate planning experts Robert A. Esperti, Esquire and Renno L. Peterson,

Esquire, the National Network of Estate Planning Attorneys is the culmination of over four decades of practical experience. Well-known estate planning attorneys and authors on the subject, they have combined their technical expertise with the skills for developing sound client relationships.

The National Network of Estate Planning Attorneys supports its member attorneys on a variety of levels, including:

- Educational and teaching opportunities.
- Support from scholars and practitioners.
- Practice development strategies.
- Practice management techniques.
- Technology enhancements to increase productivity.

LIFESPAN™ LEGAL SERVICES, LLC

Lifespan™ is a specific implementation of the Three Step Strategy™ discussed in Chapter Two. There are approximately 45 participating law firms whose attorneys are also members of the National Network of Estate Planning Attorneys. A Lifespan™ law firm is one which is committed to providing clients with an estate planning process and experience that is rivaled by no others. In addition, the implementation has been structured so that clients and their families utilizing the services of any Lifespan™ firm, anywhere in the United States, would have a similar experience. Educational opportunities for Lifespan™ families are available at any Lifespan™ firm. Our firm, Hoyt & Bryan, LLC, is a charter member of the Lifespan™ organization, and our policies and procedures are consistent with those of other Lifespan™ firms.

All Lifespan™ law firms promote fully funded estate plans, ongoing client and family education, plus a formal updating and maintenance program for the estate plans they have designed. This "maintenance" program is characterized by monthly newsletters, advanced estate planning workshops, educational programs to train successor trustees and beneficiaries, Community Builder™ programs and a biannual restatement of estate planning documents to ensure that plans are consistent with the law as well as the experience of all the Lifespan™ attorneys. Word-processing amendments to estate plans, telephone calls, educational workshops and funding assistance are included at no additional charge. The focus is on counselling, not word processing. When the time comes to administer or settle an estate (either at disability or death), Lifespan™ attorneys are committed to fully disclosed and controlled settlement costs. The number of Lifespan™ families in the United States continues to grow.

C H A P T E R 8

Ways to Memorialize Your Pet

Remembering a loved pet can take many different forms. Some of us will be satisfied with memories, others with pictures. Still, there are some of us who will want to make a special statement about the love we have for our pets. In a recent edition of *Kindred Spirits News*, a publication from the Kindred Spirits memorial program of The Humane Society of the United States, the front cover recognized a young girl, seven-year-old Savannah Williams, who was inspired to produce a CD entitled *I See You in the Stars at Night* in memory of her Golden Retriever, Gage. Anything you do on behalf of your pet's memory will be special. Here are some other ideas:

Buy a cremation urn or a memorial stone.[1] After your pet has died, the knowledge that your pet is close and safe can be a great comfort as you come to terms with your loss. Presently, the ashes of my pets Beau and Bandit are in my at-home office. I take solace in knowing they are with me at all times. If you want to memorialize your pet in this way, you have lots of choices. There are many different shapes, styles and price ranges of cremation urns and memorial stones from which to choose. Burial markers or stones can be a distinct way to mark your pet's final resting place. Lillian Vernon, a popular catalog company, now offers a memorial stone that can be personalized with your pet's name and in inscription.

Plant a tree, shrub or flower. A tree or some kind of plant makes an excellent memorial and is a living tribute to the memory of a departed friend. One of my clients told me about his mother's "garden" for the cats she has known over her lifetime. Each plant represented something special about the departed cat. For example, a pet named Lilly could be memorialized with a plant of the same name. Use your creativity to memorialize your special pet.

Spend time with friends or members of a pet-loss support group. Spending time with people who you care about, who care about you and who can relate to your loss can distract you from your pain and the anguish you are experiencing. Share your feelings of pain and loss with family, friends or if needed, a pet-loss support group. You may be surprised to discover that others have been deeply impacted by the loss of your pet as well.

Make a scrapbook or memory book. You may find solace in creating a memorial scrapbook of your favorite photos and memories of your departed pet. Your memory book can then be browsed through or shared with others as part of your healing process. Include memorabilia or other items that provide happy thoughts of your pet.

Write a poem, short story or song. Poems, short stories and songs can be very soothing during times of grief. One of my friends has a song for each of her pets which incorporates the letters of the pet's name. They are funny, nonsensical songs, but provide her with comedic relief when remembering her pet.

Celebrate your pet during National Pet Week or on Pet Memorial Day. A popular e-card web site shows the second week in May as National Pet Week. The International Association of Pet Cemeteries has designated September 10 as Pet Memorial Day. Use these dates or a special day you create to remember your pet in your own way. Other things you might consider are participating in a ceremony sponsored by your local pet cemetery, volunteering in an animal shelter or donating money in your pet's name to an organization dedicated to helping animals.

Make a charitable contribution. You can recognize and memorialize the loss of your pet by helping other pets and animals. Choose a favorite organization and make a donation in your pet's name. Charitable organizations rely on your generosity to fund the programs and services they support.

PET BURIAL AND CREMATION

People have been memorializing their pets since at least the Egyptian times, and perhaps before. We have all heard stories of cats found in the unearthed tombs of famous pharaohs. For many people, the traditional placing of a departed friend or pet in the earth by burial is the only conceivable option. There is great comfort in putting a pet to rest with its favorite blanket, toys and pictures of its family. For young children who have not experienced death and may not understand its implications, a private family-attended "pet funeral" can help explain the absence of your pet. Most of us probably have some childhood memory of attending the funeral of a family pet. I have personally conducted numerous ceremonies for departed hamsters, fish and lizards.

Cremation of your pet at death is another option. Cremation is a process whereby a pet's body is consumed by intense heat reducing it to a fine ash and bone fragments. Once cremated, you could retain your pet's ashes in an urn in your home or choose some other means for memorializing your pet.

Whether you elect to bury your pet or have your pet cremated, your pet's final disposition is a personal decision only you can make. Choose what you feel will provide you with the most lasting comfort.

Listed below are some of the burial options you might consider:

Home Burial. If you have sufficient property and there are no local ordinances prohibiting the practice, burying your pet in your yard or somewhere on your property, close to its family, can be very beneficial for all concerned. Having your pet "at home" can provide years of comfort to you and your family. The burial spot can be marked by a memorial stone or with a living tribute to your pet such as a plant, shrub or tree.

Cremains Burial. This is the burial of your pet's ashes or "cremains" after your pet has been cremated. Your pet's cremains could be placed in an urn or other appropriate memorial container. Some people have suggested burying your pet's favorite items along with your pet. A cremains burial may be the best option for those who cannot have a home burial because of local restrictions or ordinances, or for those who lack sufficient property, live in an apartment or prefer a portable memorial that can be taken if they move.

Communal or Group Cemetery Burial. This is the burial of your pet in a group plot with other pets. This is a common choice for many pet owners as it is relatively inexpensive when compared to a private burial. Both pet cemeteries and some humane organizations may offer this burial option.

Private Cemetery Burial. Your pet is buried in a private or semi-private burial plot. If desired, you could choose to bury one or more of your pets in the same plot. The cost of a private burial can vary greatly depending on the cemetery, its location and the types of services provided or desired. Upon investigation, I discovered that the services and pricing options for private burial are as varied as the number of pet cemeteries available in this country.

Like burial, there are several cremation options for your pet. You may elect private cremation with the cremains returned to you or communal cremation with or without the return of the cremains. As an alternative to burying your pet's cremains, you may elect to scatter your pet's cremains or maintain them in a memorial urn in your home or special place.

For more information on pet cemeteries, burial and cremation options, you can contact the International Association of Pet Cemeteries at (518) 594-3000. They can also provide you with guidelines for the operation and regulation of pet cemeteries.

There is a popular Internet web site, www.petloss.com, that maintains valuable information on pet memorials, pet remembrance activities, stories, poems and other activities you can participate in to remember your pet. The web site tells the story of the Rainbow Bridge, reprinted here:

Just this side of heaven is a place called Rainbow Bridge.
When an animal dies that has been especially close to
someone here, that pet goes to Rainbow Bridge.
There are meadows and hills for all of our special friends
so they can run and play together.

There is plenty of food, water and sunshine, and our friends are warm and comfortable.

All the animals who had been ill and old are restored to health and vigor; those who were hurt or maimed are made whole and strong again, just as we remember them in our dreams of days and times gone by.

The animals are happy and content, except for one small thing; they each miss someone very special to them, who had to be left behind.

They all run and play together, but the day comes when one suddenly stops and looks into the distance. His bright eyes are intent; His eager body quivers. Suddenly he begins to run from the group, flying over the green grass, his legs carrying him faster and faster.

You have been spotted, and when you and your special friend finally meet, you cling together in joyous reunion, never to be parted again. The happy kisses rain upon your face; your hands again caress the beloved head, and you look once more into the trusting eyes of your pet, so long gone from your life but never absent from your heart.

Then you cross Rainbow Bridge together....

—Author unknown

---

1   Some of the memorial ideas identified in this chapter can be found at www.foreverpets.com.

N O T E S

Pet Loss and Grief Therapy

This is an extremely difficult chapter to write. The research alone had me in tears on a number of occasions. However, if I feel this strongly about the subject of pet loss, I have to believe there are many other people who do too.

You will develop a unique relationship with every pet you will ever own. That is the great thing about pets, each is an individual that impacts our lives in different ways. Some of our pets will come to us when they are young and helpless, allowing us time to bond with them throughout the different stages of their growth. Some of our pets will be adopted or become part of our family as young adult pets or as fully mature pets. The developmental stage of your pet may influence your willingness or ability to develop a special bond with your pet. The relationships we experience with our pets will be different from the relationships we experience with people. Our pets will love us in a way that people cannot; profoundly and unconditionally. They are always supportive, never talk back and are generally ready, willing and able to join us in any activity we choose. We will love them in a way we may not love people—they will always be completely dependent upon us for all of their basic needs—like a young child. As a result of this complete dependence on us, we develop an extraordinary bond. Therefore, when our pet dies it has a deep and traumatic effect on our lives. Unfortunately, most of our pets have relatively short lives—we may have already outlived a number of pets. I expect I will outlive most of the pets I have today.

The thought of losing any of my pets is devastating to me. Yet I know that someday, unless I die first, I will experience the loss of one or more of my pets. I have already lost several pets in my lifetime and every single time it was an excruciating loss.

The loss of a beloved pet is difficult under any circumstance. However, some people, like the elderly, may experience the loss of a pet with a greater magnitude than a younger person. The older person may have already lost those people that represented the most significant relationships in their lives, especially if they have already lost their spouse, siblings or their children. If the older person lives alone, with their pet as their only companion, the loss of their pet may intensify the feeling that their house is too empty, too quiet or too lonely.

Far too often as pet owners we are called upon to make life and death decisions for our pets. Sometimes the kindest thing we can do for our pet if it is very sick, severely injured, old or even dangerous is to ask our veterinarian to humanely induce death through euthanasia. The decision to euthanize your pet is a personal one, but not one that has to be made alone. Your veterinarian, family and friends can help you make an informed decision. Because our pets cannot speak for themselves, we have to consider all of the factors affecting the quality of our pet's life in making this difficult, but sometimes necessary decision.

MAKING THE EUTHANASIA DECISION— HOW WILL I KNOW IT IS TIME?

Euthanasia is the act of inducing a humane death in an animal. Euthanasia is defined by Webster's New Collegiate Dictionary as "the act or practice of killing or permitting the death of hopelessly sick or injured individuals (as persons or domestic animals) in a relatively painless way for reasons of mercy." The term euthanasia is derived from the Greek terms *eu* meaning good or easy and *thanatos* meaning death—in other words, a good or easy death, preferably with minimal pain and distress.

Anytime we induce the death of a pet, it should be done with respect and with as little pain and distress as possible. The timing, location, presence of the owner and other factors can influence the amount of distress experienced by a pet during the euthanasia process.

The request to euthanize a pet is not a decision to be taken lightly. All of the factors should be considered including:

1) **The current quality of your pet's life**—is your pet eating well, still playful, affectionate, able to respond in normal ways, abnormally quiet, tired or withdrawn? Is this quality of life likely to change for the better? Will it get worse?

2) **Is your pet in pain?** Is there anything you can do to make your pet more comfortable?

3) **What are the treatment options that are available?** What are the costs—both emotional and financial?

4) **Do you still love your pet in the same way?** Are there any feelings of resentment or anger that your pet is interfering in your lifestyle, playing havoc with your budget, or affecting your ability to eat, sleep or work?

Your veterinarian can help you make the decision to euthanize your pet, but cannot make the decision for you. You have to understand all of the factors affecting your pet's condition. If you determine that your pet is no longer able to respond to you in usual ways, is experiencing extreme pain, is terminally ill or critically injured, or the financial or emotional cost is beyond your means or ability to endure, the time may be right.

Once the decision has been made, you need to consider the timing, location and your presence during the euthanasia process. You may want to have your pet euthanized at home or you may feel more comfortable at the veterinary clinic.

If you choose to have your pet euthanized at home, you may have to schedule the appointment either first thing in the morning or last thing in the evening. Your veterinarian may have an additional charge for a home visit. What will you do with your pet after the euthanasia process? Will you bury your pet at home or will your vet arrange for the cremation or final disposition of your pet?

If your pet is to be euthanized at your veterinarian's office or clinic, you may want to consider the circumstances under which the procedure will take place including the timing of your appointment, whether you may be required to wait in the waiting room, your willingness to be present and the final disposition of your pet. If you intend to bury your pet at home, you must be prepared to take your pet home with you.

Other difficult decisions include how you will say your final goodbye if you elect not to be present during the euthanasia process. You should also consider whether you will want to be alone or whether you will have a friend or family member present. Will someone be available to drive you home?

The final disposition of your pet must also be considered. Will your pet be cremated or buried? Has your vet requested permission to conduct an autopsy in the event the circumstances of your pet's death were unclear? Will your veterinarian handle the final disposition arrangements or will you handle these details personally?

There are many critical decisions that must be made— none of them easy. If you have the luxury of time and can make these decisions in advance, you can discuss all of the options available to you with your veterinarian. If an emergency situation requires immediate action, these are important decisions to consider now.

WHAT CAN I EXPECT—
WILL IT BE PAINLESS?

When your pet is euthanized, death will come quickly and painlessly. A death-inducing drug is administered—generally an overdose of an anesthetic, possibly pentobarbital, so that your pet stops breathing and then dies quietly and without pain or consciousness. Typically, your veterinarian will clip some hair from the front of your pet's leg and make the injection into a vein in that leg. It takes only a few moments for the drug to take effect. Occasionally, a second injection may be given into a kidney or the heart.

In some instances your pet's muscles may relax or contract after your pet has died. This can be upsetting if you are not prepared for this possibility in advance. Rest assured, your pet is not aware of these things since they are taking place after death.

SHOULD I BE PRESENT
DURING THE EUTHANASIA PROCESS?

This is a very personal decision that will depend on your emotional tolerance and individual preference. Many people feel this is the ultimate gesture of love and would not dream of permitting their pet to pass without the warmth and comfort of their owner. However, there are some people who will prefer not to experience the loss of their pet while they are present. If you do not feel you can be present, you should not feel like you are abandoning your pet. Your veterinarian and their staff will be with your pet and can provide comfort in your absence.

If you decide to stay with your pet, you may need to decide whether you will be there alone or whether other family members (including children) or friends will be present. The decision to have children present will depend on the age and maturity of your children along with family attitudes toward death. You and/or your family may want to have time alone with your pet prior to the procedure. Share your decisions in advance with your veterinarian so that proper arrangements can be made.

I was present for the euthanasia of both Beau and Bandit. It is certainly not a situation I wish to repeat many times in my life. However, in both cases, I was able to hold, stroke and comfort my pets until the very end. It seemed an appropriate gesture to accompany my pets on their final journey. I would not have wanted them to face that journey alone.

WOULD YOU EVER EUTHANIZE A HEALTHY PET?

There are circumstances when you may decide to euthanize a healthy pet. Your pet may suffer from extreme behavior problems to the extent that it has become dangerous, unmanageable, or difficult to maintain. In addition, economic, emotional and other limitations (such as space if you have a large animal such as a horse) may force an owner to consider euthanasia if a suitable home cannot be found in the event of disability or death. Some people may prefer to euthanize their pet rather than inflict the stress of a new home or family in the event of the owner's death. Discuss all possible alternatives with friends, family and your veterinarian so that you can feel comfortable with your decision.

HOW DO I EXPLAIN MY DECISION TO MY CHILDREN?

Many factors will influence how a child will feel when a pet dies. Often children have a special relationship with pets. The age and maturity of your children may determine how and when you tell them about your decision to euthanize the family pet. Generally, children will respect straightforward, truthful and simple answers. Experts have suggested it is counterproductive to tell children that the pet is being "put to sleep" or "has been taken by God." Both of these explanations can create unreasonable fears in the mind of a child. Some children may thereafter be afraid to go to sleep at night or develop a conflict resulting in anger at God for the perceived cruelty inflicted on the pet. Very young children may feel that the loss of the pet may be

138

related to something they have said or done. For this reason it is important to explain they share no responsibility for the loss of the pet and that the pet has simply died and will not return. Some children will expect that death is temporary and their pet will return. It is important to explain to children that death, although permanent, is not a disease and will not result in their own death.

A funeral or memorial service for your pet that your child has an opportunity to help plan and participate in can facilitate understanding and acceptance for your child. Children are capable of understanding and comprehending that death is a normal and acceptable part of the life cycle.

HOW CAN I SAY GOODBYE?

Farewells are always difficult. It is impossible to simply "replace" a loved one—especially a beloved pet with whom you have shared unconditional love. For this reason, the act of saying goodbye will be important in dealing with your feelings of grief, sorrow and your sense of loss. If you feel you have lost a friend, companion or family member— you have.

Find a special way to say goodbye to your pet—one that provides you with comfort and provides a natural sense of closure. Choose one of the suggested ways to memorialize your pet in perpetuity.

HOW CAN I FACE THE LOSS?

After your pet has died, it is completely normal to feel sadness, sorrow and even guilt. You may feel that you have somehow failed in your duty and responsibility to your pet—to provide them with an environment that was safe and free from danger, pain and fear. If your pet dies from a terminal illness you may feel there was something more you could have done to try and save your pet's life. This is especially true if your pet was ill for a period of time before the cause of illness was discovered. If your pet dies from a natural disaster or an accident, you may blame yourself for permitting harm to come to your pet or for your inability to prevent the circumstances that caused the accident. When a pet dies from natural causes such as old age, it doesn't make the loss any easier.

THE GRIEVING PROCESS

Grief is a journey, not an event or destination. We all experience grief when we experience a loss. It is a normal, natural, physical and emotional response. Your reaction to the loss of a loved pet can manifest itself in many different ways. Grief can result in feelings of hopelessness, helplessness and guilt. Although grief can be extremely painful, it is a necessary part of the healing process.

People experience grief in many different ways. The way you experience a loss will be different from the way someone else may experience the same loss. Some of the factors that contribute to the ways we experience grief include our value systems, religious beliefs, personality, family culture and life experience with loss. Other factors that will affect the way you experience the loss of a loved one are:

Your Age. Your age will influence the way you grieve and process the feelings of loss.

Gender. It is true that men and women experience loss differently. They also grieve differently based on long-standing stereotypes of acceptable ways to grieve. Men are expected to be strong, not to cry and not to express their emotions openly. On the other hand, it may be perfectly acceptable for a woman to be more emotional, cry openly and share their feelings with others.

Your Support System. Do you have friends and family that can provide emotional support and understand the magnitude of your grief? Will your co-workers understand the depth of your loss? In our society, although our employer may provide bereavement leave for the loss of a family member, this same policy may not apply to the loss of a pet, despite the fact that our sense of loss and sadness may be just as significant.

Your Financial Resources. What effect did the long-term care costs and commitment to provide medical services for your pet have on your financial resources? Many times people embark on a course of medical care that is significantly beyond their financial means in an attempt to "do everything possible" to save their pet. If the pet dies, the net result can be overwhelming medical bills.

Your Health. Are you in good physical health? If you are suffering from an illness at the same time as your pet, it may have an effect on our ability to work through the grieving process.

Other Resources. Do you belong to a church, social organization or have other opportunities to interact meaningfully with others who can provide emotional support during your time of loss?

THE STAGES OF GRIEF

Grieving is a complex process

The stages of grief tend to be universal and are experienced by everyone who suffers the loss of a loved one. Grief may manifest itself in a recognized sequence of stages or may appear as a complex series of emotions and feelings. The time a person spends in each of the grieving stages will be different for each person and may depend on environmental factors. Once a stage of grief has been experienced it does not mean that stage can not be experienced again or in another sequence.

The stages of grief for the loss of a pet are the same as the stages of grief for the loss of another family member. You may experience, denial and isolation, anger and/or guilt, bargaining, depression, sorrow or sadness, and finally resolution and acceptance.

Denial and Isolation. Our initial reaction to bad news is to deny it. We may not believe what we are hearing. It seems impossible to comprehend that we have lost a loved pet—that our pet will no longer greet us enthusiastically upon our return home or nicker when we enter the barn, or rub up against our leg at meal time. We may experience shock, numbness and disbelief.

Anger and/or Guilt. This stage often follows denial. You may experience anger at yourself, family members, friends, your veterinarian or even your pet. You may even feel betrayed by your pet or your veterinarian. At this stage you will be searching for all of the ways in which you may have prevented the illness or injury experienced by your pet. You may be enraged by the injustice and unfairness associated with the loss of your pet.

Bargaining. We may try to strike a bargain with God if only our pet can be spared. Other forms of bargaining may be to promise our pet that if it recovers we will never or always do a certain thing again (ie. scold the pet, leave the pet, love the pet unconditionally, etc.).

Depression, Sorrow or Sadness. This is the stage most often associated with the grieving process. At this stage the pain of your loss may be at its most intense. You may find you are unable to eat, sleep, work, think, play or experience any joy. This is the stage where you should seek the support of others and the time when you should share your sorrow with others.

Resolution and/or Acceptance. This is the final stage of the grieving process. Resolution, acceptance and recovery begins when thoughts of your pet move from the front of your thoughts to the background. Images of your pet no longer occupy your mind full-time. You can finally think about the happy memories you had with your pet. Life looks a little brighter. You may be considering a new pet. You have now accepted the notion that you will always have your pet—perhaps not in its physical form—but in your heart.

I FEEL SO BAD

The physical, emotional, psychological and spiritual pain you are feeling is certainly normal. One of the most important things you can do is to be honest about your feelings. You have a right to feel bad—someone you loved deeply has died. Hiding your feelings or isolating yourself from friends and loved ones will not make your pain go away. Instead, express it. Do whatever it takes—cry, scream, rage. Do what helps you most.

WILL MY OTHER PETS EXPERIENCE GRIEF?

Often the emotions of our pets mirror our own. You may discover that your other pets stop eating, playing or interacting in familiar ways when a pet in your household dies. To help ease the grief your pets may be experiencing it is important to keep their routines as unchanged as possible. In addition, you should not reinforce negative or unwanted behavior by unintentionally rewarding grief-induced behaviors. This may be the time, however, to provide your pets with more attention and love to reinforce their feelings of safety and security.

A 26-year-old horse that belonged to one of my friends died recently. This particular horse had been an "aunt" and surrogate mother to the two remaining horses. My friend expressed that both horses reacted very noticeably to the loss of their long-time friend. In fact, she experienced feelings of guilt that perhaps she hadn't permitted her horses the appropriate opportunity to say goodbye.

SHOULD I GET ANOTHER PET?

Getting another pet is not the right answer for everyone. You may need more time. You may never want another pet. A new pet may not be able to take the place of a departed pet—it will certainly have a different personality, will not have the same shared history and may prove to be a disappointment. If you have children, the decision to get another pet should be a family decision. If all family members are not ready emotionally to accept a new pet, those family members still grieving may feel that the deceased pet was unimportant or not valued as a member of the family.

When my sister lost her puppy, Teddy, in an automobile accident, my mother was devastated. She explained she felt like she had a hole in her heart. Sometimes a new pet can help to fill that hole even if the new pet can never completely replace the lost pet.

Years ago, when my family lost our first dog, Misty (age 11), our family reaction (especially my mother's) was to take a stand against having another dog. Soon, however, my sister brought home an adorable puppy, K.D. (Karen's Delight), who quickly helped to fill the hole in our hearts. Although Misty and K.D. both shared some German Shepherd heritage, they didn't really look alike. However, it didn't take long before we were attributing characteristics of K.D. to Misty and vice versa, almost as if one became an extension of the other. At times, it was as if we never lost Misty at all. K.D. lived a long, happy life of 15 years. Today, her successor in my parent's hearts is Shana, an energetic, wonderful border collie mix.

For me, adopting Kira, my German Shepherd mix (notice a trend here?) after the loss of my beloved dog Bandit helped tremendously. I knew I would get another dog, and another love; I just didn't know when or what. I only knew I didn't want a puppy. Famous last words!

One day at a local pet fair I found her, a new child to love. She was skinny, bedraggled and tired. She had been picked up that morning from the local pound. She had been handled all day by well-meaning potential adopters and their children. She was ready for a break and a new home. One look was all it took before I was filling out the adoption application and writing a check. I was also leaving the next day for an extended business trip—I broke the news to Joe from the cell phone on the way home. Today, Kira (also known as Stinky by Joe) is one of our greatest treasures. We tell people she is a rare breed of "Chuluota dingo dog"—she looks like a German Shepherd, but in miniature. She is blonde (like her mother) with black points. I think she is incredibly beautiful and smart. She spends her days chasing and eating bugs, carrying her "baby" around the yard, relocating my shoes, terrorizing Corkie and steering clear of my horses. She is wildly energetic, sometimes playfully ferocious and extremely silly. We love her with all our hearts.

REMEMBERING YOUR PET

Death is part of the life cycle. It cannot be avoided, but its impact can be met with understanding and compassion. Try to recall the good times you spent with your pet. By remembering the happiness and pleasure of those times, you can realize and accept that your pet was worthy of your grief. You may want to establish a memorial like those discussed earlier in honor of your pet. .

From a personal perspective, I recently lost two beloved pets. Beau, a 21-year-old Siamese-mix cat I had since college. He was, and is, my longest-running relationship to date. He was my friend, my confidante and most certainly my child. I knew that losing him was going to be one of the hardest things I would ever face and, when the day came, would be one of the worst days of my life. Beau

147

was extremely healthy throughout his lifetime. At one time he weighed as much as 14 pounds. I always said as long as he was eating he would be fine. Over the years, he eventually slimmed to around 10 pounds. Eventually, the day came when he was no longer willing to eat. Even when he was only six pounds, I could not give up. Several days later, I knew in my heart the end had arrived. I called my veterinarian and asked whether he would be willing to come to my home to euthanize him. Somehow, I did not want to take Beau to the vet's office. I felt like there would be greater peace, for me and for him, if he could remain at home. My veterinarian kindly agreed to come to my home, but was unavailable until the next evening, a Tuesday night. Tuesday dawned, and the love of my life was so sick I could not bear to wait until that evening. I had to take him right then. I called the office, asked the staff to call my veterinarian and tell him I was on my way. Would he please hurry? He rushed to the office and met me there.

Because I arrived prior to his regularly scheduled appointments, my vet was able to spend about an hour with me after the euthanasia procedure. It was the worst day of my life, but one I have survived to share. I am grateful I was there and grateful I could make the decision (although many times I prayed that God would take that terrible decision out of my hands). I was able to hold Beau till the end and then spend another hour stroking his fur, telling him how much I loved him and how much he would be missed. It makes me cry today, even as I write these words. There will never be another cat, friend or child like him. He was more human than cat. He went on walks with me, slept with me, ate with me, studied with me, spent sleepless nights with me, comforted me when I was sad, made me laugh, and caused me worry, aggravation and expense. Every minute was worth it and I would do it again.

The other loss was my beloved Bandit, a Sheltie-German Shepherd mix rescued from a local humane society in 1986. He was a stray that had been mistreated. It took him years to believe he wasn't going to be beaten every time someone picked up the newspaper or spoke in a loud voice. He would do anything you asked: You just couldn't ask too loudly. He was sweet and kind with liquid brown eyes you could drown in. He was extremely happy and loved to play soccer. He liked to chase a soccer ball with the neighborhood kids out in the street. He never met a ball he did not like and could not pop. He also loved to "sing," swinging his head back and forth as he let the world know how happy he was. All you had to ask was, "Bandit, are you a good dog?" and he would rejoice. We also taught him a quieter, more controlled version, which he was happy to "mutter" when asked, "Bandit, what does the baby say?" He was a dog that loved to walk, and was devastated if left behind. In his last year, he had a "doggy" stroke and could no longer enjoy his walks. However, he still did his best to follow me out to the barn every day. The end is never what you would expect, especially this time. I came home one day, not in a particular hurry, and pulled into the garage. My brown dog lay on the brown carpet and I never saw him. Sadly, I broke his hip. He had already suffered so much with his stroke, I couldn't ask this of him too. With great sadness and tremendous guilt, my wonderful vet encouraged me to send him to heaven with a gift of love and kindness. There are times I regret that decision still.

Coping with the loss of a pet can be as devastating as coping with the loss of any loved member of our family. You should place great emphasis on learning and coping with the stages of grief: denial, anger, guilt, depression, resolution and acceptance. There are many resources and a number of organizations that can assist you in coping with this loss.

WAYS TO COPE WITH
THE LOSS OF YOUR PET

Experts have suggested many different ways to cope with the loss of your pet. Some of them include: eating a well-balanced diet, getting plenty of sleep, having a good cry, spending time with family, friends or a pet-loss support group and speaking openly about your feelings. Other things you can do are:

1) **Contact one of the many pet-bereavement resources available today.** These valuable resources can provide information regarding support groups, grief counselors and 24-hour hotlines, just to mention a few of the services available. One such service is the Association of Pet Loss and Bereavement located on the Internet at

www.aplb.org, by mail at P.O. Box 106, Brooklyn, New York 11230, or by phone at (718) 382-0690.

2) **Join a pet-loss discussion group or support group in your area.** Your local veterinary school, veterinarian or humane society should be able to provide you with a pet-loss discussion group in your area. If there are none close to you, consider starting one. The Internet is also a good place to locate a grief counselor or support group in your area. Do not be ashamed to admit you are in pain after the loss of your dear friend and companion.

3) **There are also pet bereavement counselors dedicated to your concerns related to the loss of your pet.** A pet bereavement counselor can provide individualized counseling to help minimize the impact of the loss of your pet. There are many people who understand that pets are members of our family and they provide a special kind of love. Seek out a counselor who shares this same philosophy and has a caring way of expressing this concern to you.

4) **There are a number of helpful books available on pet loss, death and grief, both for adults and for children.** Check with your local bookstore, librarian or veterinarian, or check the Internet for references.

Each person will experience the loss of a pet differently. Seek out the services that help you feel better. Create memories of your pet that will provide you with comfort for years to come. Remember, all of our pets are waiting at the Rainbow Bridge.

NOTES

Pet Memories

*This chapter is dedicated to a selection of stories,
poems, quotes and memories of cherished pets.
For others, visit www.petloss.com on the Internet.*

"HOYT PET MEMORIES"

The Story of Frosty and Dickers

Frosty and Dickers were two of my childhood dogs. Frosty, also known as "Frobear," was adopted from a local humane education shelter. She was part Poodle and part Schnauzer—a Schnoodle. Frosty was one of the cutest puppies I ever saw, but not very attractive as an adult, except to my youngest sister, Julie. Julie adored Frosty and carried her around wherever she went. I used to tease her that Frosty would never learn to walk because she had never been given the opportunity to practice.

Frosty had a pretty good life until two tragedies struck; she was kicked by my horse and she was hit by a car. Both incidents left their mark—Frosty suffered from epileptic attacks for the balance of her life. However, she took medication that provided relief and was smart enough to realize that without it, she would have a seizure. Everyday, Frosty would remind you to give her a pill and would even eat it out of your hand!

Frosty lived until she was thirteen but not without incident. When she appeared to be on her last leg, Frosty was hospitalized at a local vet's office. Julie, not willing to give up, made a last visit to see Frosty. As she entered the room, Frosty raised her head and wagged her tail. Julie bundled her up, took her home and she survived—on the love and faith of her owner—another five years.

Dickers was an Australian Terrier rescued from an Indiana humane society by a friend. However, he was unable to keep Dickers as a result of his inability to blend with the other terriers in his home. Not surprisingly, while passing through Indiana to a Michigan family vacation destination, Dickers joined our family. On one of the very first days we had him we spent many hours searching for him along the shore of Lake Michigan. He decided to go for a run, a long one. We finally found him many miles away.

Dickers had the most endearing way of begging for food. I swear his bottom was completely flat and he could sit up for hours. We loved him dearly and therefore, every time he begged, we fed him—too much. More than once he suffered from a slipped disc in his back. We would then make him a special bed, carry him outside to do his outside business and put him on a diet. When he slimmed down and his back was healed, he was always good as new.

Dickers never understood that he was a small dog. He would regularly challenge our neighbor's male Golden Retrievers to a game of war. Unfortunately, he always lost. He would end up with stitches or some other war wound. He never did learn his lesson and as soon as he was healed, would be right back over at the fence asking for more.

Princie the Pony — What a Great "Surprise"

My whole life I dreamed of owning a horse. Thankfully, my father and mother made that dream come true at age 10 when I received Julep as a "gift" from a friend. The only condition was that if I ever wanted to find her another home, she went back to her original owner. The same was not true for Princie. Princie was a chestnut and white Shetland pony. He was tiny and hairy. He also had really bad teeth—he could have definitely used a set of braces! When Princie came to live with us his name was really Surprise, at least that is what we were told. However, my mother had a pony as a child named Princie. Therefore, Surprise became Princie. He never seemed to mind.

No one ever knew how old Princie really was. Our veterinarian estimated age 30 based on the condition of his teeth. Princie was a challenge to feed as he had a very difficult time chewing his food. He always managed, but had to make "soup" first. All the other horses had to be tied so that Princie could have ample time to eat his dinner.

When small children rode Princie he was the perfect gentleman. When older children rode Princie he always gave them a thrill. We trained him to rear on command (not a good idea in hindsight) and to run from the far end of the pasture back to the house. He always knew the difference between someone who would appreciate his antics and someone who wouldn't. Princie trained many of the neighborhood kids to ride. After we rode him for several years, he went to live with our neighbors who had younger children. They rode him for years and then passed him to another neighbor with small children. Princie loved children and they loved him—he was the favorite pet for many families and lived a long and productive life.

Sammy the Cat

Sammy was my first cat. My mother will tell you that Mr. Moo was my first cat but he was really my mother's cat. Sammy was the first cat I could call my own. He was a big long-haired yellow cat. He loved to have his tummy rubbed—but only for so long. Before too long he would grab my arm with his front legs and kick the daylights out of it with his back legs.

In those days, I believed all cats were girls and all dogs were boys. Go figure. Anyway, Sammy was a boy, despite what I believed. He always went on our family vacations but hated—and I mean hated—riding in the car. He would let out the most blood-curdling sounds you ever heard. Yet we continued to" torture" him year after year, dragging him off to one vacation spot after another.

On one trip, with four kids in the car, a mother cat with four kittens and Sammy, we headed from Indiana to

Michigan. This was to be Sammy's last vacation with our family. At a roadside stop, Sammy escaped from the over-loaded station wagon. He ran into a nearby, heavily wooded area. I feel sorry for my father to this day. He had four little girls (five, if you include my mother) crying and pleading with him to find Sammy. All this, to no avail. No amount of searching or pleading was going to entice Sammy to rejoin our circus.

From a nearby picnic table, this scene was observed by a local trucker. He said he stopped at this park on a regular basis. He told my father that if he found Sammy, he would keep him and give him a good home. I have always believed he did just that.

Pepper "Lucy"

My mother's favorite cat was a black calico named Pepper. My mom, however, never has just one name for her cats so Pepper became Pepper Lucy Poosey Mother's Moosey. Kelly became Kelly Belly Bushy Tail. Murdaugh became Murt. Ashley is Ashley Lou Lou. Muffin is known as Muffin Puffin. Apparently this trait is prevalent all around the country, not just in my home, because most of my friends seem to call their cats by multiple names. I am also guilty. Beau was always Beaubus won Kanobus or Beauby. Beijing is sometimes Beechy and Cuddles becomes Cuddle Wuddles.

However, this story is about Pepper. Before my father joined The Humane Society of the United States and Pepper was spayed, we enjoyed a number of litters of kittens. Pepper was famous for providing us with a new set of kittens—always four—one for each of us—just before we were leaving on our summer vacation. Without fail, we would load up Pepper and her new kittens and take them with us. Her kittens always seemed to spend the first few weeks of their lives travelling in the car. Hopefully, this is training that may have come in handy for future owners. The kittens were always so much fun. We each had our favorite that we named and then played with constantly.

We only kept one of Pepper's many kittens—Buffy, an absolutely gorgeous long-haired orange and white kitten. When Pepper was pregnant, my mother rolled out the second story window to let her in and accidentally knocked her off the ledge! I am convinced that all of Buffy's deficiencies can be attributed to this incident. Buffy was beautiful but not too smart. She was also completely limp. You could do anything to her. She would allow you to dress her in doll clothes and would then lie in the baby carriage for hours, never even attempting to escape. At a local cat show she took first place not only because she was beautiful but because she was absolutely docile. While many of the other cats were very unhappy about the long day, the judging and the heat, Buffy took it all in stride.

Buffy never learned to use a kitty litter box, a trick most kittens are born with instinctively. This caused everyone in my family great distress, especially my mom in our new house with white wool carpets. It also gave my father a great surprise when he discovered on alternate occasions that she had used the toaster and the stove as her chosen toilet! It was also the last straw. Buffy, often admired and loved by our housekeeper, found a new home.

Again, this story was about Pepper, sort of. Pepper was much loved and lived to be eighteen before she passed away from natural causes.

"LESSONS I LEARNED FROM OL' YELLOW DOG"

By Barbara Anne Eagan
(reprinted with permission)

Yellow Dog came to my farm three years ago skinny and hairless and covered with fleas. He looked quite alarming and I shooed him away. Despite his bedraggled appearance, he scared me. His arrival coincided with my at-home vacation, and when I first saw him I was painting the pasture fence.

Each day he would come to the gate; each day I would shout, "Go away!" On the fifth day, given his emaciated appearance, I decided I had better feed him and contact the pound. I got a blanket and a bowl and called to him. He bounded over, rolled excitedly on his back, and politely (but with great enthusiasm and tail wagging) ate the cheap dried food I offered. Then he gave a great blissful sigh. He smelled to high heaven, but I gave up on calling the authorities. I made him a bed in my barn. I thought I would clean him up, doctor him, and find him a permanent home, and so time passed.

Yellow Dog became a big, beautiful dog with fluffy cream-colored hair and a strong, sturdy body. His sweet face always looked studious given his thoughtful wrinkled brow. I advertised him in the classified as a direct descendant of "Old Yeller." People actually called to ask if he really did have such an illustrious ancestor. But he found no home through my marketing plan. Mine therefore became his.

Yellow Dog took on the job of guarding the barn and the horses. When a stranger even thought of placing a hand on the pasture gate he would bark his great yodeling bark. He did his guard job well, with diligence and dignity. Yellow Dog took his job as a family companion just as seriously as he did guard duty. Never once did he show a spark of jealousy toward the privileged yard dogs, but played with them gleefully during visiting hours before dinner. Then he would quietly return to his barn stall for the night. He kept the horses company while I worked, he gave the cats something to think about besides their food dish, and he would sit quietly by my side and listen as I would tell him about my accomplishments and my sorrows—although he could not possibly have had any frame of reference or interest. If it was time for the doctor or a bath he bore it graciously. If I needed company he would go for a ride to the store with me sitting stock-still and upright in the passenger seat. He rode in the tractor cart and sat patiently as I picked oranges or did chores. He greeted my friends joyously and treated their children gently. He scared the socks off strangers when they heard his yodel and saw his size. He kept his territory well marked (and in fact gained a modicum of local fame for this). He injected joy into mundane events and became a favorite of the neighbors. He was loyal and dedicated and a good, good dog.

On March 4, Yellow Dog died in his sleep. He died as he lived by causing little or no trouble for me (except the sorrow of his loss). I chose to share Yellow Dog with you because in reflecting on his life I found important lessons for ours.

Obviously Yellow Dog believed in persevering to reach his goals, he believed in a balanced life, in the importance of getting past first appearances, in doing even small tasks to the best of one's ability, and in showing no judgment or envy. He made the effort to demonstrate his love and appreciation for those he held dear often and amply. I wish I could be a little more like him.

GREAT HORSE QUOTES

"God forbid that I should go to any heaven where there are no horses."

—*R.B. Cunningham-Graham*

"There is something about the outside of a horse that is good for the inside of a man."

—*Sir Winston Churchill (1874—1965)*

CAT AND DOG THOUGHTS

What is a Cat?
Cats do what they want.
They rarely listen to you.
They are totally unpredictable.
They whine when they are not happy.
When you want to play, they want to be alone.
When you want to be alone, they want to play.
They expect you to cater to their every whim.
They are moody.
They leave hair everywhere.
They drive you nuts and cost an arm and a leg.

Conclusion: They are tiny little women in fur coats.

What is a Dog?
Dogs lie around all day, sprawled on the most comfortable
    piece of furniture in the house.
They can hear a package of food opening half a block away,
    but don't hear you when you are in the same room.
They can look dumb and lovable all at the same time.
They growl when they are not happy.
When you want to play, they want to play.
When you want to be alone, they want to play.
They are great at begging.
They will love you forever if you rub their tummies.
They leave their toys everywhere.
They do disgusting things with their mouths and then try to
    give you a kiss.

Conclusion: They are little men in fur coats.
Which are you married to?

—Anonymous, from the Internet

Appendix A

**SAMPLE LANGUAGE FOR
WILLS AND LIVING TRUSTS**

SAMPLE ONE

Animal Care Trust

1) Background information. (Insert state name, if appropriate)
   Statutes (Insert section numbers) provide the opportunity for individuals to create a trust for the care of designated pets or domestic
   animals and the animal's offspring in gestation.

   I wish to provide for the care and financial support for the feeding, watering, grooming, housing and veterinary care of my
   pet(s). My pet or domestic animal(s) now living is/are:

   Type of Pet(s)   Name(s)

   Any references in this Article to "my Pets(s)" is/are to this/these
   named animal(s), or any pet I own at the time of my death (or disability), as well as any of my pet's offspring in gestation at the date
   of my death (or disability).

2) Care of My Pet. Following my death (or during any period when,
   in the opinion of my Disability Panel, my personal physician or
   pursuant to a court determination, I am incompetent, incapacitated or disabled due to illness, age or other cause that results in my
   inability to adequately care for my Pet[s]). I appoint
   _____ as caregiver ("Caregiver")
   of my Pet(s). My Caregiver shall make all decisions regarding the
   location where my Pet(s) shall live, the diet, exercise, (breeding),
   (training) and veterinary care of my Pet(s) as applicable.
   (OPTIONAL: If _____ cannot act as Caregiver, then I
   appoint _____ as an alternate Caregiver.)

My Caregiver is given full and complete control and authority regarding veterinary care and treatment of my Pet(s), including euthanizing the animal after first determining from a licensed veterinary practitioner that the injury or disease of my Pet will impair the quality of life of my Pet including, but not limited to, sustained, severe, life-threatening and terminal injuries, terminal illness, aged condition or temperament. I hold my Caregiver harmless from any action or claim against my Caregiver based on my Caregiver's decision regarding veterinary care and treatment made as provided in this paragraph.

My Caregiver shall be responsible for obtaining from a licensed veterinarian an annual statement of health and well-being of my Pet(s) to present to my Trustee as a means of monitoring the health and condition of my Pet(s).

(OPTIONAL: I do not want my Pet[s] used for medical research or educational purposes during life or following death [or disability].)

3) Gift to Trust. Upon my death (or disability), I give the sum of $_____ to _____ as my Trustee to be held IN TRUST, in a trust known as the _____ Trust ("Animal Trust").

4) Beneficiary of Animal Trust. The beneficiary or beneficiaries of the Animal Trust shall be my Pet(s) as defined herein.

5) Administration of Trust. Until the Termination Date, my Trustee shall, from time to time, distribute as much of the net income or principal, or both, of the Animal Trust as my Trustee determines advisable to provide for the health, maintenance and support of my Pet(s) under the Animal Trust.

The distribution may be paid to my Caregiver or by direct payment to the provider for the expenses of my Pet(s).

No portion of the principal and income may be converted to the use of my Caregiver or my Trustee, other than for reasonable Caregiver fees, Trustee fees and expenses of administration, or to any use other than for the trust's purposes or for the benefit of my Pet(s) under the Animal Trust.

6) Termination Date. The Animal Trust shall terminate when none of my Pet(s) covered by the Animal Trust are living. Upon termination, my Trustee shall transfer the unexpended trust property to _____ (insert the name of an appropriate animal-centered charity), as the remainder beneficiary, to be used for its general purposes (or other purposes as stated).

7) Enforcement of Trust Provisions. My Caregiver shall have the authority and duty to enforce the intended use of the principal and income of the Animal Trust, including the obtaining of equitable relief from the appropriate court in the jurisdiction where my Pet(s) is/are located. However, if my Caregiver is also acting as my Trustee, any remainder beneficiary under this Will/Trust may enforce said income and principal provisions of the Animal Trust.

8) Applicable Law. This Animal Trust and the Trustee shall be subject to the laws of the State of _____ applying to trusts and trustees, now in effect or as amended. Any property held in the Animal Trust or the trust itself shall not be subject to any statutory or common law rule against perpetuities.

SAMPLE TWO

Distribution of Trust Share for My Pet

The trust share set aside for (our dog, our cat) named _____, hereafter referred to as my Pet, and shall also include any other pets I own at the time of my death, shall be held, administered and distributed as follows:

Section 1. Distribution of Trust Share for My Pet

This distribution is for my Pet and applies to and is intended to provide for any pet(s) I may own at the time of my death or the death of the last of myself and my spouse.

All special and personal information about my Pet is listed on the attached Schedule A, hereby incorporated by reference.

I direct my Trustee to pay, as an administration expense, all expenses associated with the care, feeding and housing, including veterinary costs, of my Pet for the duration of its life, whether or not these expenses are deductible for estate tax purposes.

Section 2. Trustee's Guidelines

a. General Considerations

My Trustee may house or provide for housing, support and maintenance of my Pet or any other living animals that I may own.

My Trustee may·contract and pay the expenses of proper veterinary care and treatment for my Pet.

My Trustee should ensure that my Pet receives medication and proper shots when necessary to maintain good health.

My Trustee should also ensure that my Pet is not left outdoors in unusually cold or wet weather. My Pet should be kept inside during inclement weather (add other instructions as desired).

If I have left additional instructions attached as Schedule A, these instructions shall be incorporated and included in this Section.

b. Provide a Caregiver

My Trustee may hire a caregiver, hereafter the Caregiver, to provide my Pet with proper care and housing. The Caregiver shall serve at the pleasure of my Trustee and shall not acquire any "ownership interest" in my Pet. My Trustee shall have the full power and authority in my Trustee's sole discretion to remove my Pet from the Caregiver anytime my Trustee believes the Caregiver is not providing tender and loving care. The Caregiver shall be entitled to fair and reasonable compensation for the services rendered. The amount of compensation shall be an amount equal to the customary and prevailing charges for services of a similar nature during the same period of time and in the same geographic locale. No Caregiver shall base their fee upon a percentage of the trust income.

c. Early Termination Based on Cost

If the care and maintenance of my Pet shall become unreasonably expensive or burdensome for the Caregiver, my Trustee may (irrevocably) transfer my Pet to a substitute caregiver who is willing to care for and maintain my Pet in a kind and loving way.

Section 3. Provisions for Caregiver Bonus

Option 1.

My Trustee is authorized to pay an annual bonus of $_____ to the Caregiver of my Pet for each year care is given. The bonus is to be paid at the end of the year.

Option 2.

My Trustee is authorized to provide an appropriate bonus, from this trust share, to the Caregiver if my Pet should die a natural death due to old age. No bonus shall be paid to the Caregiver if my Pet dies due to accident or illness caused by the Caregiver's neglect or willful misconduct.

Section 4. Trustee's Placement

My Trustee may place my Pet with one or more of the following caregivers who agree to care for and treat them as companion pets:

Name, residing at _____

Name, residing at _____

My Trustee shall have the discretion to select one of the persons named above to receive my Pet as its Caregiver. If none of the named persons are willing or able to take care of my Pet, my Trustee shall have the discretion to give my Pet to another person or persons who agree to care for my Pet and to treat my Pet as a companion (or member of their family).

My Trustee is authorized to pay each person, selected by the Trustee, fair and reasonable compensation for accepting the responsibility as a Caregiver and to provide for my Pet.

My Trustee shall make every effort to ensure that my Pet is never used for medical research or product testing or painful experimentation under any circumstances. After placement with a Caregiver, my Trustee should make follow-up visits on a regular basis to ensure that my Pet is receiving proper care in my Pet's new home.

Section 5. Humane Shelter Placement (Perpetual Care Organization)

My Trustee shall place my Pet with the following [name of shelter], address of shelter, hereafter the Humane Shelter.

I request that the Humane Shelter take possession of and care for my Pet for the duration of my Pet's lifetime.

(Optional: or search for a good home for my Pet. Until a home is found for my Pet, my Pet should be placed in a foster home rather than in a cage at the shelter. If it is necessary to keep my Pet in a cage while making arrangements to find a permanent home, in no event should my Pet stay more than a total of two weeks [or other time period] in a cage.)

My Pet should always receive appropriate veterinary care, as needed.

If the Humane Shelter cannot locate a permanent home for my Pet within 30 days, the Trustee should be notified. My Trustee should then assist and attempt to find a permanent home for my Pet.

If, and only if, the Humane Shelter is in existence at the time of my death and is able to accept my Pet for the duration of my Pet's life, I give $____ to the Humane Shelter. If the Humane Shelter is unable to accept my Pet, my Trustee shall endeavor to locate one or more similar charitable organizations as the Trustee shall select, subject to the requests made above.

Section 6. Ultimate Arrangements

My Pet shall be delivered by my Trustee to a suitable person for temporary holding.

My Trustee shall make a reasonable cash payment from my trust assets to cover the cost of temporary care and feeding expenses for my Pet. This amount shall not be less than $_____ per day (Author's Note: Be careful here).

My Trustee shall advertise or otherwise make best (or diligent) efforts to find a permanent loving home for my Pet, taking a reasonable amount of money for this search from the Trust.

If no home can be found after _____ days, my Pet shall be taken to a qualified veterinarian to be euthanized by the most humane

method the veterinarian has competency to use. (Optional: This
option should be an option of last resort only.)

Section 7. Distribution on the Death of My Pet

Option 1.
If my Pet should die before the complete distribution of this trust
share, the trust for my Pet shall terminate and my Trustee shall distribute the balance of the trust property equally among the other
beneficiaries named in this Article.

Option 2.
If my Pet should die before the complete distribution of this trust
share, the Trust shall terminate and my Trustee shall distribute the
Trust property to (charitable organization).

SAMPLE THREE — IN THE EVENT OF THE OWNER'S DISABILITY

Provide for My Pets

My pets are important members of my family. During any period of time
that I am disabled, my Trustee, at their sole and absolute discretion, shall
provide as much of the principal and net income of my trust as is necessary for the love, care, health, maintenance and support of my pets.

SAMPLE FOUR — IN THE EVENT OF THE OWNER'S DEATH

Specific Gift of Pets

If I own any pets at the time of my death, such pets shall be distributed by my Trustee to those persons I have designated in a separate
writing (which shall be incorporated by reference) and who are willing and able to accept and care for my pets in a manner similar to
how my pets were cared for during my life.

In the event my Trustee is unable to place my pets in a loving
home, my pets shall go to [Animal care organization] and shall be

provided for in the manner described below and/or as set forth in a separate writing, which shall be incorporated by reference.

If my pets are distributed to [Animal care organization] in accordance with this Section, it is my intent that my Trustee cooperate with [Animal care organization] in finding a permanent adoptive home for each of my pets. It is my desire that the adoptive home be with individuals who will provide a loving home determined to be in the best interests of each pet I may have. My Trustee shall have the sole and absolute discretion to provide a cash bequest to the person, persons or organization adopting my pet in an aggregate amount of ($_____) or in such amount as my Trustee shall determine is appropriate considering the circumstances, per adoptive home, not per pet or animal. My Trustee may request the assistance of the [Humane Society] in addition to any other agency or charity in accomplishing my goals expressed herein.

My Trustee, whenever possible, should defer to [Animal care organization] in making a determination as to the suitability of a particular adoptive home, or any other course of action concerning my pet as authorized herein. If my pet is not be placed in an adoptive home within a reasonable time, my Trustee may cause my pet to be euthanized if no other reasonable alternative exists, in the sole and absolute discretion of my Trustee.

The balance of the trust share set aside for [Animal care organization], after first accomplishing my goals as set forth above or in my separate writing, shall forthwith terminate and my Trustee shall distribute all undistributed net income and principal to [Animal care organization], outright and free of trust.

S A M P L E   F I V E

Pet Trust

Creation of Trust for My Pet(s)— Pursuant to the provisions of (insert statute reference) of the (insert state name) Statutes, I direct my Trustee to establish a Trust in the amount of $_____ for the benefit of my dog, Rover. The Trust is to be held and administered as a separate trust for the care of my pet under the terms of this Article.

Custody and Distributions— I hereby direct that the caregiver for my pet be the person or persons identified in a memorandum for the distribution of personal property that I may leave at the time of my death. If no such person is identified or such memorandum does not exist, I direct that my Trustee place my pet in a home or homes where my pet will receive proper care. I direct that my Trustee make payment to the person or persons providing such care to my pet from the principal and income of these funds, as my Trustee shall see fit in their sole and absolute discretion. If a home cannot be found for my pet, my pet shall be placed in a professional animal care facility, the cost of which shall be paid from the income and principal of the trust. I designate (insert name) as the person to enforce the provisions of this trust.

Guidelines— Without in any way limiting the discretion of my Trustee regarding distributions of income and principal from this trust, or the placement of my pet subject to this trust, I declare to my Trustee that the primary purpose of this trust is to provide a warm, caring and loving environment for my pet for the remainder of its life, including good nutrition, exercise and veterinary care and attention. Preservation of principal is not as important as these objectives.

Remainder Interest— Upon the death of the last survivor of my pet(s), any remaining principal and undistributed income shall be distributed to my descendants, *per stirpes* (or alternate beneficiaries).

Contingent Provision— It is my intention that this trust shall be valid under the present (insert state name) Probate Code, as well as any future changes in such Code. Therefore, it is my intention that my pet, as covered by this trust, shall be considered the measuring life under any Rule Against Perpetuities, if such becomes necessary to validate this trust. If such trust shall fail for any reason, I direct that the funds be paid outright to the caregiver of my pet or pets, as the case may be, in equal shares.

SAMPLE SIX

Specific Distributions of Trust Property

1) Our Dog Buddy

Upon the death of the second of us to die, our trustee shall distribute our dog, Buddy, to (insert name A), or if he is unable or unwilling to accept Buddy, to (insert name B). If none of the above are able or willing to accept Buddy, Buddy shall be distributed as our other pets provided in Section b, below. If any of the above-listed persons accepts Buddy, our trustee shall make a lump sum distribution of $20,000 to them to compensate for the maintenance and support of Buddy.

2) Other Pets and Animals

If my spouse and I own any other pets or animals at the time of the death of the survivor of us, our Trustee shall distribute our pets and animals to those persons willing and able to accept and care for our pets and animals in a manner similar to how our pets and animals were cared for during our lives. If our pets and animals are distributed to a person under this paragraph, we additionally direct our Trustee to distribute $_____ to the person(s) accepting the care of our pets to help offset the costs of such care.

Should our Trustee be unable to provide loving homes for our pets and animals, our pets and animals shall go to a suitable animal care organization and shall be provided for in the manner described below.

If our pets and animals are distributed to an animal care organization in accordance with this Section, it is our intent that our Trustee cooperate with the animal care organization in finding a permanent adoptive home for each of our pets or animals. We desire that the adoptive home be a loving environment selected with the best interests of each pet or animal in mind. Our Trustee shall have the sole and absolute discretion to provide a cash bequest to the person, persons or organization adopting our pet in an aggregate amount of $_____ or less per adoptive home, not pet or animal. Our Trustee may request the assistance of the animal care organization, in addition to any other agency or charity, in accomplishing our goals expressed herein. If the animal care organization assisting in the placement of our pets is a qualified 501(c)(3) organization, our Trustee may distribute a cash gift of $_____ to such organization.

172

Appendix B

GLOSSARY OF TERMS

Administrator Person named by the court to administer a probate estate. Also called an Executor or Personal Representative.

Ancillary Administration An additional probate in another state. Typically required when you own assets or real estate in a state other than the state where you live that is not titled in the name of your trust or in the name of a joint owner with rights of survivorship.

Basis What you paid for an asset. Value used to determine gain or loss for income tax purposes.

Co-Trustees Two or more individuals who have been named to act together in managing a trust's assets. A Corporate Trustee can also be a Co-Trustee.

Corporate Trustee An institution, such as a bank or trust company, that specializes in managing or administering trusts.

Disclaim To refuse to accept a gift or inheritance so it may be transferred to the next recipient in line. Must be done within nine months of the date of death.

Durable Power of Attorney for Financial Matters A legal document that gives another person full or limited legal authority to act on your behalf in your absence. Valid through mental incapacity. Ends at revocation, adjudication of incapacity, or death.

Durable Power of Attorney for Health Care A legal document that gives another person legal authority to make health care decisions for you if you are unable to make them for yourself. Also called Health Care Proxy, Health Care Surrogate, Medical Power of Attorney or Advance Health Care Directive.

Fiduciary Person having the legal duty to act for another person's benefit. Requires great confidence and trust, and a high degree of good faith. Usually associated with a Trustee or Personal Representative.

Funding The process of re-titling and transferring your assets to your Living Trust. Also includes the re-designation of beneficiaries to include your Living Trust as a beneficiary.

Inter Vivos Latin term that means "between the living." An *inter vivos* trust is created while you are living instead of after you die. A Revocable Living Trust is an *inter vivos* trust.

Irrevocable Trust A trust that cannot be changed or canceled once it is set up. Opposite of Revocable Living Trust. Can be created during life-time or after death.

Intestate Dying without a Will.

Joint Ownership When two or more persons own the same asset.

Joint Tenants with Right of Survivorship A form of joint ownership in which the deceased owner's share automatically and immediately transfers to the surviving joint tenant(s) or owner(s).

Living Trust A legal entity created during your life, to which you transfer ownership of your assets. Contains your instructions to control and manage your assets while you are alive and well, plan for you and your loved ones in the event of your mental disability, and give what you have, to whom you want, when you want, the way you want at your death. Avoids guardianship of the property and probate only if fully funded at incapacity and/or death. Also called a Revocable Inter Vivos Trust.

Living Will A legal document that sets forth your wishes regarding the termination of life-prolonging procedures if you are mentally incapacitated and your illness or injury is expected to result in your death.

Personal Representative Another name for an Executor or Administrator.

Pour Over Will An abbreviated Will used with a Living Trust. It sets forth your instructions regarding guardianship of minor children and the transfer (pour over) of all assets owned in your individual name (probate assets) to your Living Trust.

Power of Attorney A legal document that gives another person legal authority to act on your behalf for a stated purpose. Ends at revocation, incapacity (unless it is a durable power of attorney) or death.

Probate The legal process of validating a Will, paying debts and distributing assets to beneficiaries after death.

Probate Estate The assets owned in your individual name at death (or beneficiary designations payable to your estate). Does not include assets owned as joint tenants with rights of survivorship, payable-on-death accounts, insurance payable to a named beneficiary or trust, and other assets with beneficiary designations.

Probate Fees Legal, executor, court and appraisal fees for an estate that requires probate. Probate fees are paid from assets in the estate before the assets are fully distributed to the heirs.

Spendthrift Clause Protects assets in a Trust from a beneficiary's creditors.

Successor Trustee Person or institution named in a trust document that will take over should the first Trustee die, resign or otherwise become unable to act.

Testamentary Trust A Trust in a Will. Can only go into effect at death. Does not avoid probate.

Testate One who dies with a valid Will.

Trust Administration The legal process required to administer trust assets after incapacity or death. Includes the management of trust assets for the named beneficiaries, the payment of debts, taxes or other expenses and the distribution of assets to beneficiaries according to the trust instructions. Generally requires the services of an attorney.

Trustee Person or institution who manages and distributes another's assets according to the instructions in the Trust document.

Will (or **Last Will & Testament**) A written document with instructions for disposing of assets after death. A Will can only be enforced through probate court.

Appendix C

SAMPLE SPECIAL DURABLE POWER OF ATTORNEY

STATE OF _____

COUNTY OF _____

I, (insert your name), currently residing at (insert your complete address) do make and appoint (insert name of agent)(hereinafter my "Agent"), whose address is (insert complete address of agent), as my true and lawful attorney-in-fact to do and execute any or all of the following acts or things:

I am the owner of the following pet(s):

(Insert pet names and description)(e.g., Bandit, my 14-year-old Sheltie mix)(hereinafter individually or collectively referred to as my "Pet").

ARTICLE 1—GENERAL GRANT OF POWER

From time to time, it will be necessary for me to leave my pet in the care and custody of my Agent. I hereby give my Agent full permission and authority to:

1) Give consent for emergency veterinary treatment as needed by my Pet in the event I cannot be immediately reached at the time of the emergency. The determination of the need for such care may be made by my Agent.

2) To authorize all necessary veterinary treatment, including surgery or hospitalization, for my Pet while in the care of my Agent. Further, my Agent is authorized to take any and all other necessary actions to provide for the safety and welfare of my Pet.

3)   To perform any and all acts, as fully to all intents and purposes as I might or could if personally present, to include but not limited to the feeding, care, maintenance and supervision of my Pet.

GIVING AND GRANTING unto my Agent full power and authority to do and perform all and every act, deed and thing whatsoever that is necessary in the execution of this Durable Power of Attorney as fully as I might or could do if present and acting. I hereby ratify and confirm whatsoever my Agent shall do in the premises by virtue of this authority.

I FURTHER DECLARE that any act or thing lawfully done hereunder by my said Agent shall be binding on myself and my heirs, legal and personal representatives, and assigns, whether the same shall have been done either before or after my death, or other revocation of this instrument.

THIS DURABLE POWER OF ATTORNEY will not be affected by my subsequent incapacity except as provided in (insert state statute reference). It is my specific intent that the power conferred on my Agent will be exercisable from the date of this instrument, notwithstanding my later incapacity, except as otherwise provided by statute.

ARTICLE 2—THIRD-PARTY RELIANCE

Any third party may rely upon the authority granted in this Durable Power of Attorney until the third party has received notice as provided by (insert state statute reference), as amended from time to time.

FURTHER, to induce any third party to act hereunder, I hereby agree that any third party receiving a duly executed copy or facsimile of this power of attorney may act hereunder, and that revocation or termination hereof shall be ineffective as to such third party unless and until actual notice or knowledge of such revocation or partial or complete termination of this Durable Power of Attorney by adjudication of incapacity, suspension by initiation of proceedings to determine incapacity, or my death shall have been received by such third party in accordance with the requirements of law. I, for myself and my heirs, executors, legal representatives and assigns, hereby agree to indemnify and hold harmless any such third party from and against any and all claims that may arise against such third party by reason of such third party having relied upon the provisions of this Durable Power of Attorney.

ARTICLE 3—NOTICE

Notice is effective if in writing and served on the person or entity to be bound by such notice by any form of mail that requires a signed receipt or by personal delivery as provided in (insert state statute) for service of process. Service is complete when received in accordance with Section (insert state statute reference).

ARTICLE 4—DAMAGES AND COSTS

In any judicial action regarding this Durable Power of Attorney, including, but not limited to, the unreasonable refusal of a third party to allow my attorney-in-fact to act pursuant to the power, and challenges to the proper exercise of authority by my attorney-in-fact, the prevailing party is entitled to damages and costs, including reasonable attorney's fees, as provided in (insert state statute reference).

Executed (insert date).

Signed, sealed and delivered in the presence of:

Witnesses   Print Name of Principal:

_____   _____

Print Name

_____

_____

Print Name

_____

(INSERT NOTARY ACKNOWLEDGMENT PROVIDED BY STATE STATUTE)

About the Author

Peggy is the oldest of four daughters born to John A. Hoyt and Gertrude "Trudy" M. Hoyt. She was born in Dearborn, Michigan, and spent her first 10 years as a "PK," or "preacher's kid," before her father joined The Humane Society of the United States in 1970. Peggy and her sisters, Karen, Anne and Julie, grew up with cats and dogs, hamsters, gerbils, fish, lizards and snakes. At age 10, Peggy and the rest of the Hoyt family moved to Maryland and Peggy got her first horse, Julep. This was a defining moment in Peggy's life. Julep was a two-year-old, untrained Arabian-Welsh cross. She was a spitfire that loved to jump. She and Peggy were perfectly suited for each other.

In the summer, Peggy worked as an assistant on Charlie Iler's Thoroughbred breeding farm. For $1 an hour, she fed 50 horses twice daily and was even permitted to start some of the two-year-olds. It was during this time that Mr. Iler offered Peggy the chance to buy a well-bred mare, Vain Ruler, off the racetrack. Peggy enjoyed watching "Lady" run in her last race.

At 13, Peggy had her second untrained horse and another equine challenge. Her love for horses never faltered, but the lure of a car and a job at the mall required that Peggy temporarily abandon her ownership of horses. Julep was returned to her original owner and Lady was sold to another girl who loved horses. With the proceeds, Peggy bought her first Mustang—a 1968 Ford.

It wasn't until after Peggy graduated college—an A.A. degree from Marymount University in Arlington, Virginia; a B.B.A. and M.B.A. from Stetson University in DeLand, Florida; and a J.D. from Stetson University in St. Petersburg, Florida—and embarked on a multi-faceted, multi-directional sales, financial consulting and legal career that she was once again able to realize her dream of horses. Peggy adopted Reno and Tahoe, her wild Mustangs, in May 1997—a traumatic and significant moment in her life. Sierra, her Premarin rescue, was adopted in October 2000.

Today, when she is not working with clients in her law practice, The Law Offices of Hoyt & Bryan, LLC; speaking to audiences regarding the value of estate planning; networking with local business people; or promoting her firm in one way or another, she is spending time "playing" with her horses, her dogs and her cats and spending "quality" time with her fiance, Joe Allen. One of Peggy's favorite sayings is "I've never had a trained horse." As a result, she spends a lot of her time incorporating the techniques of well-known horse trainers like John Lyons, Pat Parelli, and Donna M. West into her daily routine. Peggy's passion is her pets—especially her horses.

Special Thanks

I would like to gratefully acknowledge all of the writers

and sources I have utilized in this book for their insight, wisdom

and inspiration. I am appreciative to all of you as we

certainly share a common bond—our love for animals, a concern

for their well-being and how we might utilize estate planning

to provide them with a secure future. Any failure to

provide proper acknowledgment or credit for the work, thoughts,

ideas and expressions of others is not intentional.

In addition, I have endeavored to determine whether previously

published material included in this book requires

permission to reprint. If there has been an error or omission

of any kind, please accept my apology and a correction

will be made in subsequent editions.